Susan Annette Muto

RENEWED AT EACH AWAKENING

The Formative Power of Sacred Words

DIMENSION BOOKS
Denville, New Jersey 07834

248
Mo R

First English Edition 1979
Published by Dimension Books
Denville, New Jersey 07834

Copyright © 1979 by Susan Muto

Nihil Obstat: Rev. William J. Winter, S.T.D.
Censor Librorum

Imprimatur: Most Rev. Vincent M. Leonard, D.D.
Bishop of Pittsburgh

June 1, 1979

L.C.C.C. # 79-54046
ISBN 0-87193-04-9

248A
mur

TABLE OF CONTENTS

PART ONE
Awakening with the Word

PART TWO
Fashioned by the Word

BOOKS BY THE AUTHOR

FOREWORD

This book is about the power of sacred words to fashion our lives in relation to self, others, and God. Part One contains reflections that emerged from a living contact with the words of Holy Scripture and the spiritual masters. Part Two deals more specifically with spiritual reading as a formative art.

I believe as we go through life certain key words have the power to make us be and become who we are. Language fashions our being from the first utterances of babyhood to the last words we speak as we pass from life. Words build human relationships or tear them down. They express the mysteries of being as well as the mundane trivia.

In this book I have tried to share some thoughts about words that have had a formative influence on my life—such words as "rhythm," "peace," "emergence," "suffering," "solitude," "silence." As I enter more and more into the experiences these words convey, I appreciate their power to transform my life. I feel grateful to the spiritual writers, poets, novelists, and essayists whose respect for the word has inspired my own love for spiritual reading, acknowledging especially in this regard the lectures and published works of Father Adrian van Kaam. In fact, I often recall these words of Dag Hammarskjöld as a guide to my own responsibility as a writer:

> *Respect for the word* is the first commandment in the discipline by which a man can be educated to maturity—intellectual, emotional and moral.
>
> Respect for the word—to employ it with scrupulous care and an incorruptible heart-felt love of truth—is essential if there is to be any growth in a society or in the human race.
>
> To misuse the word is to show contempt for man. It undermines the bridges and poisons the wells. It causes Man to regress down the long path of his evolution.[1]

I hope that this book on the formative power of sacred words will be a small step toward remembrance of that eternal message that "In the beginning was the Word: the Word was with God and the Word was God." (Jn.1:1)[2]

Language is our participation in the Divine Word; thus we must never take it lightly. The source of our speaking and writing must be that same silence from which the Eternal Word leaps forth. Only as we grow in our own capacity to live meditatively can we become channels through which God speaks. Then He can use our words to draw others into discipleship—to draw them from the darkness of deception into the light of Divine Truth. It is my intention to dedicate this book to all the persons in my life who allowed awakening to take place, especially my parents, Frank and Helen Muto.

PART ONE

AWAKENING WITH THE WORD

I

"If you understood the meaning of the text, 'It is mercy I desire and not sacrifice,' you would not have condemned these innocent men." (Mt. 12:7)

A hunter in the desert saw Abba Anthony enjoying him-self with the brethren and he was shocked. Wanting to show him that it was necessary sometimes to meet the needs of the brethren, the old man said to him, 'Put an arrow in your bow and shoot it.' So he did. The old man then said, 'Shoot another,' and he did so. Then the old man said, 'Shoot yet again,' and the hunter replied, 'If I bend my bow so much I will break it.' Then the old man said to him, 'It is the same with the word of God. If we stretch the brethren beyond measure they will soon break. Sometimes it is necessary to come down to meet their needs.' When he heard these words the hunter was pierced by compunction and, greatly edified by the old man, he went away. As for the brethren, they went home strengthened.

(The Sayings of the Desert Fathers)

I

RHYTHMS OF REFLECTIVE LIVING

Charles Dickens observed in his *Tale of Two Cities:* This is the best of times and the worst of times. His words ring true today. It is the worst of times in many ways. We cannot close our eyes to the problems we see: the lack of morality, the diminishment of values, the corruption and dishonesty that faces us daily in the newspapers. From a merely human perspective, it is difficult to make sense out of what is happening. Why have we forgotten the things we as a people and nation have valued most? Yet clearly ours is not only a human perspective. Ours is a vision of faith in which we see who we are and what we are called to do in this world with the eyes of God.

When we consider this time—that we have just labeled the worst—against the divine horizon, we can say that it is the best of times too. It is a time when we are being tested. God is asking us to undergo a purification; that means suffering and disillusion. Only then may we be able to value again the beauty of nature, the generosity of God, the good will of man. We are challenged in these best of times—no matter where we go or what we do—to be witnesses for the Christ-life in which we believe.

A banner reads: Bloom where you are planted. Wherever you are, in office or family room, wearing a white collar or blue, bloom where you are planted. Come alive. Give of your best self. Stand for what you believe in. Such dedication fills us with a sense of joy and accomplishment.

Deep down we Christians have faith in the human spirit illumined by the Holy Spirit. This faith is what we build on when the times toss us between the worst and the best. We retain the freedom to change our attitude toward the situation, despite the hardship involved. We can always say, "It's up to me to be the best person I can wherever God places me." If I give my children the love and attention they need, put good meals on the table, have some treats waiting for them when they come home from school, then I'm blooming as a mother. If I can be patient in the classroom no matter how aggravated I feel, if I can try to make this "thick head" less thick, then I'm blooming as a teacher. I'm doing the best I can and that's what God asks of me.

How can we foster in ourselves and others this blooming of life? The word rhythm comes to mind—swinging to music that we like; the rhythmical ebb and flow of the sea; the rhythms of our bodies that respond to the cycles of the season: we bask in the sunshine of a lovely spring day, but the doldrums overtake us on the "dog days" of summer or in the bitter cold of winter.

The human body is a rhythmical creation of God that flows with the rhythms of nature to which we are bound. To get in touch with my body-spirit rhythm helps me to know who I am uniquely and who God is calling me to become.[1] What is the rhythm by which I operate? How do I best respond?

There are three basic rhythms that seem to be part of the human condition: the rhythm of active and passive strength; of attachment and detachment; of humor and seriousness. These rhythms characterize the human spirit as alive in the Holy Spirit; they signal an orientation to transcendent values as manifested in the everyday.

The strength I have in mind is not the brawny type that builds muscles; it is inner strength, moral fiber. In the fullest sense it alternates between two components: one active, the other passive. What does it mean to be a strong person? Strength seems to be a question of capability to do the things we have to do. It involves keeping in touch with daily life, making sound decisions and practical judgments, incarnating realistically our inspired ideals. Strength also carries with it a passive component, one we are likely to miss in our fast-moving world. We tend to forget the need to pause, to step aside, to reflect on what we are doing. Is this action in touch with the deepest self God is calling us to become?

Without the passive component of patient endurance in situations we cannot change, strength can become mere activism. The "doing mode" overloads us with new ideas. We go along with the demands of others without paying attention to where we are in the midst of all this activity. Active strength alone wears us out mentally and physically. We rush along, often overlooking the real needs of people; in our eagerness to help we refuse to return to that center within ourselves where God guides what we should do and endure.

In his diary *Markings* Dag Hammarskjöld presents the right rhythm of active and passive strength. He took on valiantly all kinds of responsibilities, but not without bringing himself quietly before the Lord to ask:

Did'st Thou give me this inescapable loneliness so that it would be easier for me to give Thee all?

Still a few years more, and then? The only value of a life is its content—for *others*. Apart from any value it may have for others, my life is worse than death. Therefore, in my great loneliness, serve others. Therefore: how incredibly great is what I have been given, and how meaningless what I have to 'sacrifice.'

      Hallowed be Thy Name,
      Thy kingdom come,
      Thy will be done—[2]

15

The integration of striving and stilling is complemented by that second rhythm of attachment and detachment. We are attached to our friends and colleagues, our parents and peers. The human self "tacks" on to people, events and things. We do not like simply to "hang loose." We want to have a home port—some place where we can feel wanted and loved. We need to have roots somewhere and at least a vague notion of what we are going to do tomorrow and the next day. Experience tells us, however, that we also have to "de-tack" ourselves, whether we like it or not.

Every moment of detachment in our lives is like dying a little to the old self that we may arise to the new life awaiting us. With detached eyes we can see each moment as an invitation to care. Because we see persons and things as passing, we treat them as infinitely worthy of respect. Paradoxically, only when we are detached can we be present fully to the now. The rhythm of attachment-detachment thus implies that we try to care about everything and everyone with whom we come in contact because we see them as created by God and beloning ultimately to Him alone.

Lastly, we alternate in life between laughter and tears, humor and seriousness, joy and pain. In the midst of suffering, it is refreshing as Christians to experience the carefreeness of being sons of God, of trusting that He will relieve us of our burdens and give us rest. We are, of course, to take seriously our work, to carry our cross, to bear our responsibilities, but not at the expense of ceasing to be joyful.

Children have a delightful sense of humor and remind us of what we adults need to retain. I remember taking my niece to a flower show. I told her about all the beautiful greenery she was going to see and I could feel her getting excited. The exterior of the conservatory is an awesome structure, high-domed and glass-enclosed. For a little child of five, it would be frightening to enter. So, instead of spontaneously running in, she pulled back and quiveringly confessed, "But I don't want to go inside." I asked, "Honey, why not?" She looked at me with tears in her eyes and said, " 'Cause I ain't never been in a big flower pot before."

Children see things in this fresh way that delightfully blends seriousness and humor. Their example points to the life we ought to live—one that basically trusts in God, loves him, has faith, and knows that there is always in life some meaning that calls for rejoicing. Take this tale, for instance.

Once upon a time, in a solemn monastery, there lived a monk who had the peculiar trait of driving his brother monks "up the wall," for no matter what happened—whether a monk stubbed his toe, had a mystical revelation, or spread a marvelous feast on the table—he would have a scriptural quote to cover the situation. At long last his brother monks complained to the prior of the abbey about this habit which was upsetting them and disturbing their peace of mind. His penance was to kneel in utmost reverence, not smiling or laughing in any way, in the middle of the refectory where the other monks would take their noonday meal. He had to do this day after day.

One afternoon, during the quiet of their lunch hour, there came up over the side of the hill a braying jackass that had gotten untethered from the barn where it was kept. The beast caused an uproar. The prior jumped up. The monks jumped after him. "Get that jackass out of here," he shouted. "It's disturbing our peace." Meanwhile our friend in the middle of the refectory was bursting with suppressed laughter. His shoulders were shaking and his face was contorted because he couldn't get the chuckles out. After the incident occurred, the prior motioned to him and said, "My brother, come here. If you can find a scriptural quote to cover that situation, your penance is over." With a pious face, eyes raised to heaven, he turned to the right, turned to the left, looked straight in the eyes of the prior, and said: "He came unto His own and His own received Him not." (Jn.1:11)

That's what humor does. It helps us to put things back in perspective. It humbles us so that we can be the rhythmical selves we are—active and passive, caring and not caring, serious but filled with the lightheartedness that signals the liberty and joy of being a Christian.

II

"I tell you all this
that in me you may find peace.
You will suffer in the world.
But take courage!
I have overcome the world." (Jn. 16:33)

This simple truth, that the sole purpose of man's life on earth is to do the will of God, contains in it riches and resources enough for a lifetime. Once you have learned to live with it uppermost in mind, to see each day and each day's activities in its light, it becomes more than a source of eternal salvation; it becomes a source of joy and happiness here on earth. The notion that the human will, when united with the divine will, can play a part in Christ's work of redeeming all mankind is overpowering. The wonder of God's grace transforming worthless human actions into efficient means for spreading the kingdom of God here on earth astounds the mind and humbles it to the utmost, yet brings a peace and joy unknown to those who have never experienced it, unexplainable to those who will not believe.

(Walter J. Ciszek, S.J., *He Leadeth Me)*

II

LOOKING WITHIN TO FIND GOD'S PEACE

Not long ago I sat in the airport of a major city and looked at the faces of fellow passengers. They were awaiting planes, x-raying their luggage, rushing to meet late flights. I was struck by the looks of anger and frustration on so many faces. Others looked blank and inscrutable, as if they were wearing masks. I wondered if my own face registered an equally grim look. What were we running after? Money, fame, personal fulfillment?

Whatever it was, the goal seemed to elude us. Perhaps we were seeking the wrong goal. Or were we seeking the wrong way to it? Whatever we go after that promises fulfillment seems to fall short, to have about it some flaw or imperfection, however slight. The extra money we earn becomes inflated and never seems enough to cover new expenses. The higher position brings with it added duties and more worrisome problems.

It seems that as long as we focus on material or merely human reality as the source of inner peace, we are bound to be disappointed, for that goal can give only limited satisfaction. Money is spent, status changes, friendships fail. What seem to be sources of lasting happiness and peace pass shortly away. They are threatened by vulnerability. If we want to find that deep seated peace and happiness that neither moths nor woodworms can destroy nor thieves steal away (Mt. 6:20), we must attempt, with God's grace, to reconsider our goal and the right way of achieving it.[1]

Spiritual writers speak of our having a core of peace that gives us the goal and guides us in a certain direction. But where do we begin in a society that calls us to fortune and fame, that causes such distraction and agitation? Perhaps an analogy may help.

Consider a pond in winter. A skater pivoting on the ice. A solitary person practicing a Figure Eight. Turn, reverse, turn—climaxing in a vigorous yet graceful spin. The pivot ends abruptly. The young man skates off to further perfect his skill. What is the secret of such a feat? It is the skater's ability to focus on one object. As long as he concentrates on one thing—a tree, a fence, a point on the distant horizon—he will maintain his balance.

I also need a point on which to focus if I am to preserve my equanimity. As the skater's calm is not touched by his whirlwind activity, so too I need a core of peace enabling me to begin each new action with my feet firmly on the ground.

The activities of professional life can reach whirlwind proportions. The tension of nervous strain begins to affect me. Energies diffuse. The direction my life takes is unsteady. There seems to be no stopping. I experience dizziness. Now is the time to ask myself if I have lost my point of focus. If so, it is wise to fix my gaze on the Lord, the source of calming union.

To maintain a core of peace requires that I look within myself to find God, for it is around Him that my life must resolve. Such prayer gives me a chance to gather together the circles of activity in which I feel myself dispersed. I look at my involvements and try to place them in relation to God's will for me. For the sake of inner peace, I let go of peripheral concerns.

With this focus of faith, I may find that the cause of my agitation is a shift from God as center to self as center. To be most deeply at peace, I must heed the words of the psalmist and set the Lord ever before me; then I shall not be disturbed. It is only the Lord who can lay to rest our restlessness. Peace is His gift.

Peace I bequeath to you,
my own peace I give you,
a peace the world cannot give, this is my gift to you.

(Jn. 14:27)

If we receive the gift of Jesus' peace, we should see its fruits at work in us, especially in our relations with others. Jesus commanded us to love one another, even if at times we are not able to "like" one another because of lack of affinity. This commandment means that we are not only to love that anonymous mass of people on the other side of the world but that we are to try to love the person who sits across from us at the breakfast table or the one who lives next door. This struggle to love our neighbor, even though we often fail, would be the mark signifying that we were living in Jesus' peace.

St. Peter affirms this connection between love and peace in his message to the brothers.

> . . . you should all agree among yourselves and be sympathetic; love the brothers, have compassion and be self-effacing. Never pay back one wrong with another, or an angry word with another one; instead, pay back with a blessing. That is what you are called to do, so that you inherit a blessing yourself. Remember: *Anyone who wants to have a happy life and to enjoy prosperity must banish malice from his tongue, deceitful conversation from his lips; he must never yield to evil but must practice good; he must seek peace and pursue it. Because the face of the Lord frowns on evil men, but the eyes of the Lord are turned toward the virtuous, his ears to their cry.* (1 P. 3: 8-12)

As we move through life, many obstacles threaten this peace. Our selfishness may keep people and God at a distance. We become preoccupied with our business and its distractions. We trust no one and move about as if we were our own savior. These obstacles can be tempered when we are with true friends in brotherly love, for friendship calls us out of ourselves. When we share concerns with others, we transcend the confines of self-centeredness.

As we begin to feel comfortable with our friends, we also feel more at home with ourselves. If the relationship is a liberating one, each of us is strengthened to stand on his or her own feet while at the same time experiencing caring others on whom we can depend. On basis of this friendship, we ready ourselves for a deeper friendship with God and a more profound peace.

When we are with our friends, we often sense the presence of God between us. Like the disciples on the road to Emmaus, we can experience friendship as the occasion on which Jesus joins us in a special way. In the face of discouragement, these two disciples remained together. They had given up everything and fled, but they had not forsaken each other. When they held firm to their friendship, though their dreams and hopes were apparently shattered, the God they were searching for confirmed their faith.

The difficulties we encounter with our friends can teach us about ourselves. At first we may be overjoyed by the many things we have in common. We experience so much affinity. This relationship sustains and affirms the persons we are. As it begins to develop, minor disagreements may arise. We see some of our faults and feel slightly disillusioned. We may slip into moods where we become less communicative.

Many times these stumbling blocks look like the "beginning of the end," but they are really a beginning. True friendship helps to bring out the flaws in each other's personality that keep us from being our best selves. For example, what if I need to be right all the time, to have the final say in every situation? My friends help me to be sure of the abilities I do have but also to admit honestly that I am limited.

As we work through these obstacles, as we learn to forgive, we find that our friendships grow stronger. We no longer need to impress others. We care for one another in a less selfish way. We grow in respect and our love becomes more mature.

I once saw a poster that read: "A friend sees me through even when he sees through me." A friend is someone with whom I can talk about things that really concern me. I don't have to be afraid of saying something foolish. I don't have to try to be eloquent or impressive. If I did, my friends could see through the ploy anyway. They see me through a bad mood, a tough job, a trying experience. I feel their support and understanding expressed through a helping hand, a concerned confrontation, a consoling remark. My friends see me through to what I can become, no matter how I stumble along.

With my friends, I don't have to be someone I'm not, just to be liked. I can be the imperfect self I really am. My friend's affirmation does not lead me to become embedded in what I am right now. Friendship helps me to find that peace and love we see as our goal.

Growing together as friends can teach us much about growing intimate with God. When we first meet God as a Person, we may be infatuated with what promises to be a relationship of perfect peace if we continue on this road to Him. And we are right. But there are obstacles along the way too. Our love of God has to be purified if it is to last when the consolations disappear. Only if we are willing to go through the desert can we enter into deeper union with Him.

Being with our friends also teaches us to be more open, thoughtful and caring. This trustful openness allows the other to be as he is and teaches us to be more open to God. We allow God to really be God in our lives as we try to respond to the movements of His grace wherever they lead.

An obstacle to union is the burden we place on ourselves by trying too hard to be perfect at once. If we make a mistake or fail, we become anxious and tense. We are not at peace; we feel as if we have to merit by our own achievement God's gift of peace. But peace is given to us even while we feel unworthy to receive it. God is present to us in our imperfection. His love is faithful to us even when we are unfaithful to Him.

God's peace works through who we are now. He does not wait until we become who we would like to be or think we should be. He gives freely. All we need to do in gentle receptivity is to accept humbly His grace, His love, His peace.[2]

The graciousness of God can be overwhelming. It may be too much for us to take. The whole atmosphere in which we live says we have to compete for what we get. We have to earn it. No wonder we find it difficult to believe in this gift of peace. God sees through us perfectly. He sees us as we can never see ourselves—in all our weakness—yet His vision goes beyond to our deepest center, to that inner kingdom where He dwells. Though we are far from living in the image He has made, God sees us through.

Our relationship with our friends reflects our encounter with God. With our friends we are able to rejoice in the loving and lovable self God has graced us with; we are more open to receive His peace.

Friendship can thus be a facilitating condition for spiritual growth. Friends can open our eyes to the hidden goodness of others and to our own capacity. They can help us to forgive one another and to be forgiving toward ourselves as we strive to refine the rough edges of our life. In the pain that is part of any friendship, we learn generosity, other-centeredness, compassion; we learn the meaning of love in the real world of limited human beings.

To have a friend is a rare gift in life; friendship is not something we can force. Like peace, it comes to us as a gift. If we are without a friend, we need not frantically search for one; this fact can be a call to grow through solitude closer to God. Even if God gives us a friend, we must still be aware of the limited nature of human friendship compared to the limitless love of God. Friendship is purest if our love, desire and remembrance of God increases with our affection for our friends. Only then can this association strengthen our relationship with the Divine Lover and gradually help us to overcome the obstacles to His love in our life.

Indeed the lovely but limited nature of friendship makes us desirous of holding our hearts for the one love that lasts through this life and into the next, claiming and giving everything.

III

"I assure you, unless you change and become like lit-tle children, you will not enter the kingdom of God. Whoever makes himself lowly, becoming like this child, is of greatest importance in that heavenly reign." (Mt. 18:3-4)

Just as I thought I must live out my life beset by these dif-ficulties and anxieties (which in no way lessened my con-fidence in God and which only increased my faith) I sud-denly found myself changed and my soul, which up till then was always disturbed, experienced a profound interior peace as if it had found its center and a place of peace.

Since that time I have walked before God, in simplicity and faith, with humility and love, and I have labored diligently to do, say and think only what would please Him. I trust that when I have done all that I can He will do with me as He wishes.

(Brother Lawrence of the Resurrection,
The Practice of the Presence of God)

III

SELF EMERGENCE IN CHRIST

Imagine a rose bud, fresh and dewy. Hold that rose in your mind's eye for a moment. Then, as if you were filming in slow motion, watch the bud unfold. Petal upon petal, moist, fresh, beautiful. Slowly the bud blossoms into a rose.

Everywhere in nature we watch the mystery of emergence. To emerge is to unfold, to grow, to blossom forth, to become the unique self I am before God. To emerge is to change, to find the direction of my life, to pause and compose myself, to listen to what the Spirit is saying in the depths of my heart.

To emerge is not to stand still; it is to be a continuous event as we read in *The Emergent Self:*

> The emerging person is one who believes in his own plentitude and taps the source of his potential.
>
> How much more promise is in us than we suspect? Are not most of us mere caricatures of what we ought to be?
>
> * * *

No man draws on all of his resources at every moment, except perhaps in myth. Every man has some of them available. However, he never reaches a stage beyond which he cannot emerge in some way.

Thus the emergence of self is a continuous event. We never arrive; we are forever arriving.[1]

***

The adventure of emergence brings new life even if we have become zombie-like in our living. Due to the pressure of day to day, we may have lost the sparkle that enables us to appreciate little things like the blossoming of a rose or the celebration of a new birth.

The Spirit of God dwelling in us is dynamic, creative, ongoing, flowing forth. To grow in and with Him is to find out who we are—pilgrims always on the way.

Emergence involves a rich array of human experience. Children seem so tiny when they are born, yet a month later they are already growing out of their baby clothes. The sketch on the architect's drawing table soon becomes a new building. Beyond emergence on these vital and functional levels, we also develop as spirit selves in Christ. He calls us to be recreated in His likeness day by day.

Spiritual growth happens slowly, for God's time is not bound to human clocks. If it were up to us, we would like instant solutions to our difficulties, but God seems to prefer a gradual pace. As we enter into a commitment to follow Christ, we discover some patterns of emergence that foster the spiritual life. Like the slow unfolding of flowers in nature, like the hardly perceptible growth of a child, spiritual deepening is usually undulating and slow—like a dance.

My body grows; my mind expands; my spirit opens up to the Holy present in people, events and things. This dynamic process of emergence becomes concrete in daily life. We follow Christ wherever we are—in classroom or hospital, kitchen or office, science lab or symphony hall.

At certain times in our life, we may have to move to new, unfamiliar places and situations. This can be painful. We know what we are, but we don't know what we are becoming.[2] Thus in the adventure of emergence we go through a phase of alienation. We do not feel comfortable in the situation we are in; nor do we feel at home in our new surroundings. Alienation is often followed by a kind of ambivalence. We decide that we may get used to this change after all. We move from the "It's hopeless" attitude to the "It's not so bad after all." Ambivalence may then change into affirmation.

As we move from one stage of life to the next, we can take Christ as our model. Like the apostles, we long to stay on the mountain of transfiguration, but Christ calls us back to the valley of everyday where we must listen to the Father's will. Everytime we want to sit still in complacency, the Lord urges us on. St.

Augustine described this tension of rest and restlessness in his *Confessions.*

> You are great, O Lord, and greatly to be praised: great is your power and to your wisdom there is no limit. And man, who is part of your creation, wishes to praise you, man who bears about within himself his mortality, who bears about within himself testimony to his sin and testimony that you resist the proud. Yet man, this part of your creation, wishes to praise you. You arouse him to take joy in praising you, for you have made us for yourself, and our heart is restless until it rests in you.[3]

Other than resting in God there is no rest possible for man. We are all seeking the gift of oneness with God. We cannot be content to rest in either material or spiritual possessions. In the words of St. John of the Cross, "The soul that journeys to God, but does not shake off its cares and quiet its appetites, is like one who drags a cart uphill." (*Sayings of Light and Love,* #53).[4] Our restless hearts can rest only in God; then refreshed by His Spirit, we can return to our day to day task, renewed in our intention to obey His will.

Holy Scripture sheds light on this mystery of emergence in Christ by revealing a progression in relation to God from servant, to friend, to son.

"Which of you, with a servant plowing or minding sheep, would say to him when he returned from the fields, 'Come and have your meal immediately'? Would he not be more likely to say, 'Get my supper laid; make yourself tidy and wait on me while I eat and drink. You can eat and drink yourself afterward'. Must he be grateful to the servant for doing what he was told? So with you: when you have done all you have been told to do, say, 'We are merely servants: we have done no more than our duty.' " (Lk. 17:7-10)

This passage reminds us of our total dependence on God and expresses the first requirement for discipleship—namely, that as the master is, so the servant shall be:

Anyone who loves his life loses it;
anyone who hates his life in this world
will keep it for the eternal life.
If a man serves me, he must follow me,
wherever I am, my servant will be there too.
If anyone serves me, my Father will honor him.

(Jn. 12: 25-26)

And again:

I tell you most solemnly,
No servant is greater than his master,
no messenger is greater than the man who sent him.

(Jn. 13:16)

And yet so profoundly loving is the relationship between God and man that He moves us a step beyond our servant capacity to a new level of intimacy. We read of this change in John's Gospel.

A man can have no greater love
than to lay down his life for his friends.
You are my friends,
if you do what I command you.
I shall not call you servants any more,
because a servant does not know
his master's business;
I call you friends,
because I have made known to you
everything I learned from my Father.
You did not choose me,
no, I chose you;
and I commissioned you
to go out and to bear fruit,
fruit that will last;
and then the Father will give you
anything you ask him in my name.
What I command you
is to love one another.

(Jn. 15:13-16)

Jesus leads us from being servant to being friend on the condition that we do what He has commanded and that we share the fruits of this friendship with others.

Still scripture takes us a step further in this process of emergence. In the Epistle of Paul to the Romans, we read:

> Everyone moved by the Spirit is a son of God. The spirit you received is not the spirit of slaves bringing fear into your lives again; it is the spirit of sons, and it makes us cry out, 'Abba, Father!' The Spirit himself and our spirit bear united witness that we are children of God. And if we are children we are heirs as well: heirs of God and coheirs with Christ, sharing in his sufferings so as to share in his glory.
>
> (Rm. 8:14-17)

We must continue to be servants and rejoice in being God's friends, but we are all His children, sons of God through the merits of His first-born Son, Jesus. To share in His glory, we must also share in His suffering.

God offers each of us the privilege of discipleship, friendship, sonship, provided we are willing to accept all that goes with this invitation, especially the way of the cross. The cross we live need not be in the form of extraordinary physical, emotional, or spiritual suffering. Most likely it will take the form of a cold that forces us to stay in bed; of an impolite person who closes the door in our face; of a cab driver who takes us the long way home insisting it's a short cut.

All of these persons and events comprise the little crosses of everyday. The question is, how do we live them? Grumbling, complaining, feeling frustrated, or as part of Christ's call to discipleship, friendship, son-ship?

We know that emergence in Christ is a gift of grace, but we can cooperate with grace by removing obstacles and creating conditions that facilitate our readiness to receive. For example, take the symbol of hands. Tightly clenched fists represent a person im-prisoned within himself, holding on to his cares, possessions and pride. Open hands signify release of self to God, a letting go of our guilt feelings, burdens and cares so that, filled with Christ, we can begin anew to witness and to serve. In this example, our grasping must give way to letting go and trusting in God to sustain us.

Another obstacle to emergence in Christ is a greedy, mastering approach to the mystery of our life as compared to waiting in wonder as life unfolds under God's care. In his novel, *Zorba the Greek,* Nikos Kazantzakis presents the character of the Boss as a personification of this calculative approach. The Boss goes out walking one day and sees hanging from a twig a cocoon in which a butterfly is waiting to emerge. He notices at once that the cocoon is begin-ning to flutter. He gets excited. He wants to witness the miracle of new life so much that he blows his hot breath on the cocoon and increases the speed by which it opens. The butterfly comes forth but it has shriveled wings and expires the moment after it is born. The Boss had hastened God's time and killed the butterfly. He recognizes in remorse that there is another dimension to life that cannot be controlled by man.[5]

By contrast, when we surrender in wonder to the mystery of our emergence in Christ, we face reality as it is. We perceive behind the surface of things the mystery of God's presence. In discipleship, friendship and sonship we emerge as unique selves in the Lord. We go before Him with empty hands so that He can fill us with all that is good. The growth He grants fosters gifts of inner life such as being centered in God's will while living amidst the complexity of life; slowing down to enjoy "minute vacations" so we can sink our roots in the soil of life's enduring values; living in such a way that no joyful secret of God's abundant grace may be missed.

To the Father we raise our whole being, a vessel emptied of self, and pray:

> *Accept, Lord, this my emptiness,*
> *and so fill me with Thyself—*
> *Thy light, Thy love, Thy life—*
> *That these thy precious gifts*
> *may radiate through me and*
> *overflow the chalice of my heart*
> *into the hearts of all with whom*
> *I come in contact this day,*
> *revealing unto them*
> *the beauty of Thy joy and wholeness*
> *and the serenity of Thy peace*
> *which nothing can destroy.*

IV

> *"I tell you truly:*
> *you will weep and mourn*
> *while the world rejoices;*
> *you will grieve for a time,*
> *but your grief will be turned into joy."*
>   *(Jn. 16:20)*

If only kings and their ministers, princes of the Church and of the world, priests, soldiers and ordinary people knew how easy it would be for them to become very holy! All they need to do is fulfill faithfully the simple duties of Christianity and those called for by their state of life, accept cheerfully all the troubles they meet and submit to God's will in all that they have to do or suffer—without, in any way, seeking out trouble for themselves. It is this attitude which gave such holiness to those patriarchs and prophets who lived long before there were so many methods of spirituality and so many directors of souls. This is the true spirituality, which is valid for all times and for everybody. We cannot become truly good in a better, more marvelous, and yet easier way than by the simple use of the means offered us by God, the unique director of souls. It is the ready acceptance of all that comes to us at each moment of our lives.

(Jean-Pierre de Caussade,

Abandonment to Divine Providence)

IV

CREATIVE SUFFERING IN EVERYDAY LIFE

If someone were to ask you the following question, what would your answer be? From what are you suffering at this moment in your life? Thinking about it, I would most likely begin with the obvious, namely, the first source of suffering we can all identify with is bodily. We feel fatigued after a full day of work. Maybe we have a tension headache. It crawls up the back of our spine and gives us a crick in the neck. We feel a stiffness in our joints, especially if it rains or if we tend to be slightly arthritic. Maybe we get indigestion from swallowing our hamburger too quickly. Eye trouble? Difficulty with hearing or breathing? All possible. If we took a survey, how many would be on some kind of medication for the chest, the heart, the stomach, and other organs?

Clearly, one source of our suffering is due to the fact that we are *embodied* spirits. Our body has a lot to do with our suffering. The body is corruptible. And, though we may take many precautions, for instance, good nutrition, exercise and recreation, sooner or later some suffering is going to inflict itself upon us. The aches, the pains, the sheer deterioration of getting old—all reveal the body as a source of suffering.

Suffering that is linked with our body we call pain. All of us have known pain at one time or another. Even something simple can cause pain like buying a new pair of shoes and developing a blister on our ankle or toe. It can be agony when we run for our bus and our blister starts burning. We all know what it is like to suffer bodily distress.

To remedy this kind of suffering, we seek medical relief. We take an aspirin or go to the doctor for a prescription. Under normal circumstances, we can find a way to cope with bodily suffering.

There is a second kind of suffering, far more difficult to relieve, for it affects not merely the vital sphere of the self but the functional-emotional dimension. Here is a new possibility for suffering that deeply disrupts our lives. Think, for example, how we feel about a failure in our work. Despite putting forth our best efforts and zeal, we don't achieve our goal. Colleagues can neither understand nor appreciate what we are trying to do. A betrayed trust. That too causes suffering. We have truly shared something of ourself with a person and find that our trust has been betrayed in a casual way. The suffering of a broken marriage; surface friendliness that hides seething anger; repressed hostility and rage suddenly thrust at us. The suffering we feel when gripped by anxiety.

We awaken in the middle of the night in a kind of sweat. We feel afraid and don't even know what we are anxious about. Our life is half over, and there are so many goals we have not realized! We've reached the crisis of the limits. We may never realize them. Here again suffering grips us.

Clearly this source of suffering has something to do with the fact that we are *spirits* in a body. An animal might well experience the kinds of pain associated with the body, but it cannot suffer from such intangibles as failure or dishonesty or thwarted love; it does not know anger, anxiety, or the affliction of living with years of guilt. Only a human being suffers in that way. We can go on and on listing the reasons why we suffer more than bodily pain. Perhaps a rather simple way of putting it is that "our hearts hurt." We can be hurt and we do suffer, and not just because of physical ailments. The tears rush to our eyes in many situations when our bodies feel just fine. Vitally we are perfectly healthy and yet our throats struggle to hold back the tears and, worse yet, the frustration without tears.

We can refer to such functional and emotional suffering as *affliction* to distinguish it from the suffering associated with the body, that we call *pain*. Such is the affliction of Job, who cries out:

> Remember that my life is like the wind;
> I shall not see happiness again.

> (Jb. 7:7)

42

Or of the psalmist who laments:

> For I am wretched and poor,
> And my heart is pierced within me.
> Like a lengthening shadow I pass away.
>
> (Ps. 109: 22-23)

There it is: the awareness of our passing. This indeed seems to be the deepest source of human affliction. No animal, no plant knows that it is going to die. But we do and it is that knowledge which leads to a third source of human suffering we can call *spiritual*.

This suffering occurs, for example, when we experience doubt rather than faith. It is felt in dark moments of human life when we wonder with a kind of unvoiced question: Is there really a personal God? Does He care about my life? Is what I believe or claim to believe true? Especially during times when we experience bodily or emotional suffering, we open ourselves to the possibility of suffering spiritually.

The doubt, rather than the faith that has sustained us, pulses in our brain. The despair, rather than the hope we have clung to in dark hours, becomes our companion. These negative experiences of doubt and despair, even in the extreme a kind of hatred of God that may arise when we feel "done in" on the bodily or emotional level, pierce to the center of our being. They feel to us like a kind of dying, not actual, physical death but a human dying on the spiritual level. Such experiences may also occur when prayer life feels as if it is utterly drying up. We feel forsaken by God. Malaise pervades our soul and makes us cry, ''What's the use of anything after all? Life is so short. Before we turn around, we are ready for the grave! Where did all the years go?''

Such spiritual suffering can be termed *dying*. We die to so much that formerly sustained us—the passing pleasures, the treasured possessions—all of that pales in the context of the spiritual dying we now experience. We feel our nothingness. Now indeed we come to a crossroads in the human quest for meaning. It is as if we are suspended between actual death (and for some suicide seems to be the only way out) and the slowly emerging conviction that somehow out of this darkness can come new life. Here we enter into the possibility of suffering being not merely a negative but a creative experience. Perhaps at least once in our lives, however dreadful it may be, we have to come to the crossroads, when all that we counted on seems taken away, if we are to experience that out of this nothingness new life and meaning can blossom forth.

Certain authors have tried to guide us through this tangled forest of pain, affliction and dying, through this dark tunnel to the other side where a glimmer of new life and creativity seems to shine. One such author is Viktor Frankl in his book, *Man's Search for*

Meaning. In the concentration camp, Frankl felt the turning point fast approaching—the feeling of being abandoned without hope. Actual death—self inflicted or inflicted by one's captors—was one option. But was it possible to face the situation squarely and seek the option that there could be a creative thrust to these apparently inhuman events? As we know from his autobiographical account, Frankl opted for the side of creative suffering, and in so doing raised himself and others from the level of mere suffering—useless and meaningless—to that of creative suffering. He sought an answer not to the mystery of suffering itself but to a way of living it meaningfully.[1]

Our Lord in the Garden of Gethsemane prayed: "My Father, if it is possible, let this cup pass me by. Still, let it be as you would have it, not as I." (Mt. 26:39) In His prayer, Jesus shows us a way to move from the realm of meaningless suffering to creative suffering. The way is simply this: we have to accept what is happening to us, look it in the eye, and face it courageously. Then we are on the way to living its reality, even if we do not fully grasp its meaning.

In the following psalm, note the acceptance of suffering on all levels: bodily, emotional, spiritual. The psalmist recognized, as Frankl did, that even if we never find a logical answer to the mystery of suffering, it is in accepting the fact of this reality and dealing with it that we are set on the road to meaning.

Hasten to answer me, O Lord,
For my spirit fails me.
Hide not your face from me
lest I become like those who go
down into the pit.
  At dawn let me hear of your kindness,
for in you I trust.
Show me the way in which I should walk,
for to you I lift up my soul.
Rescue me from my enemies, O Lord,
for in you I hope.

(Ps. 143: 7-9)

If we hope to enter into the possibility of living our suffering as creative, we must listen to something else the text indicates. It is only when the psalmist ceases to look at himself and looks instead to God that he lifts himself out of the narrow framework of pain and affliction, death and despair, and raises his eyes to the Divine Other. Only then does there begin to dawn that glimmer of possibility that he can once more walk in the light.

The same shift in perception happened to Job. He is the biblical model of the struggle we all go through to make some sense out of our suffering. As long as Job looked at himself or listened to his friends, he got more and more confused. It was only when he raised his eyes above his plight and hearkened to the voice of God that he was suddenly lifted beyond his desperate situation and saw it against the horizon of the Divine.

When he listened to God in abandonment and faith, he saw his place in the mystery of things. He ceased trying to understand his suffering and simply listened to God. We too must attend to what God is saying to us in the midst of pain, affliction, and dying. We too must trust Him and His holy will.

> I know that you can do all things,
>   and that no purpose of yours can
>   be hindered.
>
> I have dealt with great things that I do
>   not understand;
> Things too wonderful for me, which
>   I cannot know.
>
> I had heard of you by word of mouth,
>   but now my eye has seen you.
> Therefore I disown what I have said,
>   and repent in dust and ashes.
>   (Jb. 42:2-6)

The message of suffering's meaning comes for Christians when we meditate on the death and resurrection of Our Lord. The crucifix shows us an act of utter self-emptying for our sake. Jesus Himself felt forsaken in the end, but He trusted in the Father's will. So must we. The meaning in all of this dying is that it leads to the creative moment of new life. The answer to suffering for the Christian resides in the hope and promise of resurrection. To live with the dying Christ on Calvary is to live with the risen Christ in glory. This mystery surpasses human understanding but its truth is found in faith. As St. Paul tells us:

> . . . when we were baptized in Christ Jesus we were baptized in his death; in other words, when we were baptized we went into the tomb with him and joined him in death, so that as Christ was raised from the dead by the Father's glory, we too might live a new life.
>
> (Rm. 6: 3-4)

To follow this death-resurrection cycle more concretely, it might be interesting to compare the process of creative suffering with the stages reported by psychiatrists and psychologists who study the dying process in terminal patients. They have identified for us certain phases in this experience that can be applied not only to the case of terminal patients but to any experience of suffering we undergo. These stages have been researched by teams of psychologists, by people involved in pastoral counseling programs in hospitals, and so on. Their research with terminal patients has taught them to live more meaningful lives because they, like all of us, are themselves terminal patients. We may not have cancer or kidney disease yet, but each of us is dying a little at each moment of suffering and loss. So what these researchers tell us about terminal patients can be relevant here and now, though we may live joyfully and vitally for years to come. This research has been pioneered by Elizabeth Kubler-Ross. Living with, consoling and caring for terminal patients has led her to the discovery of the following stages in the dying process.[2]

First of all, there is the stage of *denial* of the fact that one is dying. "This can't be happening to me." The same denial of the fact of suffering in any form also happens. This denial is especially prevalent in our culture due to fear and the general flight away from facing death calmly as part of the normal course of life. We wait for the bad news of a terminal disease instead of learning to die with dignity a little every day. We do not usually do so in our society. Unlike some tribal communities for whom death is integrated with the processes of life, we confine it to hospital rooms and funeral parlors, making sure there are lots of living things around the dying or dead one—flowers and, of course, when the end comes, mourners to detract from the fact that a corpse is there. We fix "it" up so "it" looks just like "it" looked when "it" was living. Though respect enters in, the danger is that our fear of facing these terminal situations will persist. We all fear the things associated with actual dying—the pills, pains, and family pressures. Hence our denial of this reality.

The researchers go on to say that denial is followed by a *partial acceptance*. The reality is there. It has happened, but acceptance is only partial because soon it is accompanied by feelings of anger, rage and increasing dismay. A turmoil is going on inside me. Accompanying the rage and anger is a sense of horrible isolation: "This is happening to *me* and no matter how many friends I have to support me, I've got to go through this tunnel alone." Death certainly evokes the pain of being alone. It takes a while before the joy of solitude can begin to emerge out of that pain. No one can walk through this dark valley for me.

A tragic sense of life pervades the person on this occasion. The eternal questions are asked: "Why me, God? Why are you allowing this to happen to me? What wrong did I do in my life to deserve such harsh treatment?" Note the emphasis is on *me* at this stage of the dying process. Because death is an interruption of *my* activities, it is an interruption of *my* nice, secure life. Now that security has been violently broken into and disrupted. Hence the questions increase: "What do others really know about what I'm going through? What do they care if I'm suffering so horribly?"

At this stage Kubler-Ross and other researchers record a third factor, that of *bargaining*. A bargaining process goes on inside one's self and with God. For instance, the person may say, "Maybe if I cease being angry at people and at God, I can enter into some sort of agreement with the Powers That Be and postpone a little the inevitable." This kind of bargaining in one sense might be likened to a prayer of petition. We pray for healing before God, knowing that He has granted this gift and forestalled what seemed a sure fate. Though bargaining may be a genuine experience of prayer, inevitably the nature of the prayer is still somewhat self-centered, based on what *I* want and what *I* think is best. The person has not yet reached the stage Jesus reached: " . . . let it be as you would have it, not as I."

Bargaining buoys one up. It gives me a sense of consolation and hope in the midst of trial and that is good, but the blow is harder to bear when the bargain does not work. That is what is bad about bargaining. Hence, bargaining, the researchers say, is often followed by a fourth stage, *depression*. The person has used his last "ace in the hole." He played that card and it did not work. It is easy to understand why that experience is followed by depression. The dying one can no longer deny his ailment. He has used up all the excuses—blamed it on others, blamed it on God, blamed it on the devil, but there is no one to blame anymore.

In the case of the terminal patients with whom these researchers work, they may be in pain on the bodily level unless under sedation. The body becomes weaker and thinner and the person can't smile away his illness. He may respond to this depression at first by going numb, by becoming rather stoic, but soon he is invaded by a great sense of loss. After all, we love our life. There is in us a tremendous inclination to preserve life. When we see that it is passing, we sense the loss of persons and things we love most in the world. The person knows he has to go away and cannot come back. At times it is crucial for the dying person to experience himself surrounded by people who love him and feel compassion for him, for example, the medical and ministerial staff, his family and friends. Knowing he can cry with these people and not feel ashamed helps to wean him slowly and gently out of that depression so he can come to the next stage.

Here intercessory prayer can be important. When we pray for the sick or for the dying, this spiritual support—even if we are not in the immediate presence of the dying person—is felt as sustaining. Many of our intercessory prayers are heard by God; He does give the person the grace to gradually accept the fact that, "Yes, I have to go away, I cannot return."

A fine text on this topic written by a Quaker author is entitled "Dear Gift of Life," and subtitled "A Man's Encounter with Death." There is a gentleness and interiority in Quaker spirituality that is quite touching. In his pamphlet, Bradford Smith records his experiences as a terminal cancer patient. On January 31, 1964, he wrote the following poem on "Matter."

How strange: these immaterial things—
House, tree and lawn,
Even this marble step, this crumbling clod—
Were here before, will be here after I have gone.

Can matter, mattering so little,
Outlast mind and spirit?
What matters most lives quick and quickly dies:
But does it leave no echoing mind to hear it?

What matters, dies, but matter lives?
What never lives can't die;
That only dies which lives—death is life's badge,
And life is death's. So I salute them all—sky,
House, tree, lawn, marble, clod.
Stay then, and let me by.[3]

Here the tone is no longer one of anger, bargaining or depression. The person begins to accept his passing and hence enters the fifth stage of the dying process: *genuine acceptance.* He senses that what is has to be and that he has to live it through. He now finds some degree of meaning and even joy in living reality as it is. By facing the situation bravely, he finds resources in himself he never knew existed. He can draw upon reservoirs of strength that surprise him. The focus is no longer so much on *my* dying, *my* fate, *my* self pity, but simply on getting one's affairs in order, writing wills, providing for the family, saying good-bye to loved ones left behind, generally feeling free. Now, in

Christ, one who is a Christian can turn more and more trustingly to the Father, Son, and Holy Spirit to whom he shall return shortly in the new life that awaits him after death. To abandon one's self in a gentle and open fashion is simply to let what has to be, be. Again from Smith:

The discovery that you have cancer is also the discovery that you are going to die. Not necessarily from this cancer, this operation, for you may still live to die of heart disease or falling down the cellar stairs. But the message now comes home, strange and yet familiar: I too am mortal.

By necessity then you are led to meditation, even if you have not been much given to it before. In the long dark hours after the hospital has quieted down, in the period when a half-departed anesthesia has left your body, and, in the surge of new life that comes with recuperation there are rich opportunities for facing what you have to face, savoring all that memory brings you as its gift, and knowing more clearly than ever before what you want to do with the rest of your life.

. . . .

I thought I would feel cut off by my illness from the rest of the human world. Instead, I found that human contacts grow warm, they glow, when you are in trouble. Family loyalties strengthen. The bonds grow firmer with friends and neighbors, and we become as one family. Distant friends somehow learn what has happened; you hear from boyhood chums with whom you had lost all contact. The grandsons who come to visit on the lawn outside the hospital window—how additionally precious are their unseamed faces, their clear voices, their handsome soundness of feature and limb![4]

Accompanying this genuine experience of acceptance is what Smith and others describe as a mysterious and yet quite commonly felt sense of oneness. Paradoxical, isn't it? The experience that seems to separate us most from others, suffering and dying, on another level, when lived in meditation, ends up granting us the gift of a sense of communion and community.

> I also found myself full of an overflowing sense of oneness, not only with all these, not only with mankind which somehow gains through suffering a sense of its unity such as it rarely gains through joy, but with all of life, whose givenness is that it must struggle to be born, struggle to live, and then surely die.
>
> A few days after the operation, the March on Washington took place. I asked to have the television set connected and watched all day. For me the great moment came when Marian Anderson, in that universal voice which so incredibly combines the earthly with the heavenly, sang: "He's got the whole world in his hands." The words, so nobly simple, expressed the whole drama of what I had been feeling. I do not cry easily, but tears blurred the image of that humbly expressive face on the screen—tears not of sorrow or even of thanksgiving, but of a sense of the fullness of life and its oneness.[5]

To see in death this potential for new life, whether or not one is a terminal patient, offers a sure indication of suffering's potential for creative living.

Thus death opens the door to life, to life renewed and re-experienced as a child experiences it, with the dew still on it.

And so comes the next opening—the sense of being part of a universe, of a personal relatedness to all life, all growth, all creativity. Suddenly one senses that his life is not just his own individual existence, but that he is bound in fact to all of life, from the first splitting off of the planets, through the beginning of animate life and on through the slow evolution of man. It is all in him and he is but one channel of it. What has flowed through him, flows on, through children, through works accomplished, through services rendered; it is not lost. Once given the vision of one's true place in the life stream, death is no longer complete or final, but an incident. Death is the way—the only way—life renews itself. When the individual has served his purpose as a channel, the flow transfers itself to other channels, but life goes on. And in this great drama of life renewed, one sees and feels the divine presence, and feels himself one with it.[6]

There are many tributes to the "Dear Gift of Life" that complement Smith's—texts from scripture and the spiritual journals of other Christians—that testify to the nobility of the human spirit which shines forth more brightly than ever on the occasion of its passing.

Dietrich Bonhoeffer, the renown Protestant theologian and spiritual writer, recorded such an experience on the eve of his execution in a concentration camp. His poem, "Stations on the Way to Freedom," parallels the process of creative suffering we have been pondering. We see unfolding in four vivid stanzas the life of a human being on the way to ultimate freedom.[7]

56

The first stage, that of self discipline, requires, he says, a certain mastery of sense and reason so that these vital-rational powers become servants of the spirit-self and instruments of the Holy Spirit. We must strive, therefore, to be pure, chaste, obedient to God and oriented toward His divine directives. Bonhoeffer writes:

> If you set out to seek freedom, you must learn
>   before all things
> Mastery over sense and soul, lest your wayward desirings,
> Lest your undisciplined members lead you now this way,
>   now that way.
> Chaste be your mind and your body, and subject to you
>   and obedient,
> Serving solely to seek their appointed goal and objective.
> None learns the secret of freedom save only by way
>   of control.

The energy of a vigorous, vital, well functioning life spills naturally over into action. In this energetic period, one lives to follow and make real his ideals. The poet says we are caught in the "tempest of living." We hear God's command and in soldierly fashion fearlessly heed it.

> Do and dare what is right, not swayed by the whim
>   of the moment.
> Briefly take hold of the real, not dallying now with
>   what might be.

RENEWED AT EACH AWAKENING

Not in the flight of ideas but only in action is freedom.
Make up your mind and come out into the tempest
of living.
God's command is enough and your faith in Him to
sustain you.
Then at last fredom will welcome your faith amid great
rejoicing.

The vital years, the incarnational years, the years when we function will soon give way to a turning point, a distinct transformation. Hands, once active and powerful, become withered and old. This is the stage of suffering. Work ends, though the deeper meaning of one's commitments remains. But now the initiative belongs to God and to Him we must yield our freedom.

See what a transformtion! These hands so active and
powerful
Now are tied, and alone and fainting you see where your
work ends.
Yet you are confident still, and gladly commit what
is rightful
Into a stronger hand, and say that you are contented.
You were free for a moment of bliss, then you yielded
your freedom
Into the hand of God, that He might perfect it in glory.

At last the curtain draws to a close. There is only one scene left to play: the fourth and final stage is death. Because Bonhoeffer is a man of faith, he calls his death the "highest of feasts." We leave behind our ephemeral body and know at last the freedom of meeting God face to face.

> Come now, highest of feasts on the way to freedom eternal,
> Death, strike off the fetters, break down the walls that
>   oppress us,
> Our bedazzled soul and our ephemeral body,
> That we may see at last the sight which here was not
>   vouchsafed us.
> Freedom, we sought you long in discipline, action, suffering.
> Now as we die we see you and know you at last, face to
>   face.

Such is the death of a noble and dignified spirit. The reflections of Smith and Bonhoeffer grant us, who still have to face that final scene, the strong conviction that through death we shall learn the meaning of the dear gift of life. Only in death do we experience the ultimate freedom and fulfillment for which our spirit yearns. Hence we move with poets and spiritual masters who have faced the darkness of death into the light of resurrection. We sense the oneness of being that is their legacy and ours in God.

Let us conclude, then, with a brief poem by Bradford Smith, entitled simply "One." On this joyful note the Christian ends/begins his journey to life.

RENEWED AT EACH AWAKENING

O God, God, God, you are everywhere—
In sun and light and rain and dew,
In birdsong, leaf shadow, and sweet breath
Of every breeze that blows;
In every child's flowered face,
In every act of human grace;
In storm and calm, in love and praise,
In the sweet progress of our nights and days;
In seasons as they come and go,
In hearthside, woodland, piling snow:

Within, without,
dissolving doubt
That all is one
Lord—of life, and death, and everlasting sun.[8]

V

The chief priests, with the whole Sanhedrin, were busy trying to obtain false testimony against Jesus so that they might put him to death. They discovered none, despite the many false witnesses who took the stand. Finally two came forward who stated: "This man has declared, 'I can destroy God's sanctuary and rebuild it in three days.' " The high priest rose to his feet and addressed him: "Have you no answer to the testimony leveled against you?" But Jesus remained silent. (Mt. 26:59-63)

God became man for the sake of man. This event is so utterly extraordinary and so much against the experience of reason and against everything the eye has seen, that man is not able to make response to it in words. A layer of silence lies between this event and man, and in this silence man approaches the silence that surrounds God Himself. Man and the mystery first meet in the silence, but the word that comes out of this silence is original, as the first word before it had ever spoken anything. That is why it is able to speak of the mystery.

It is a sign of the love of God that a mystery is always separated from man by a layer of silence. And that is a reminder that man should also keep a silence in which to approach the mystery.

(Max Picard, *The World of Silence*)

61

V

SOLITUDE AND SILENCE: THE INWARD QUEST

On basis of our own experience, we can see immediately that there is a difference between loneliness, described as the pain of being alone, and solitude as the joy of being alone.

All of us recall times when we've known the pain of loneliness. For instance, feeling alone in a crowd or being shut out by someone we love. We want so much to speak but are at a loss for words. We want to tell the other what we are going through, but he does not understand. We are never so alone as in a twosome where the other person, though loved and close to us physically, is insensitive to our simple pleasures. He cannot share the joy I feel in glancing at a sunset, chuckling at a joke, taking a quiet walk.

We experience loneliness when we are sick. Something minor may be troubling us like a headache or the flu; a general malaise may point to more serious problems. Whatever the case may be, sickness makes us feel suddenly alone. We realize again that no matter how much family members love us, they cannot make our illness magically disappear. We have to live it through alone.

Another instance of isolation can occur in old age. Most of us are fortunate because we have a family to whom we can turn. But compare the picture of human loneliness we see when we go down to the dock district of any city. Walk around the streets and see these poor senior citizens with nowhere to go, with no one to care. In them we feel the pain of isolation—that homeless feeling of being a displaced person with no sense of purpose.

These experiences of aloneness are often preceded or accompanied by disgust with ordinary routine. Things that should inspire our daily lives breed instead a bored feeling. This general loss of meaning may be due to a lack of faith, hope and love. We do not experience spiritual darkness, in which we wait faithfully for God, but the darkness of feeling utterly withdrawn and alone, isolated from others and the Divine Other.

Only when we come to grips with the pain of being alone can we understand and appreciate the joy of being alone. Such moments of solitude can lead to positive religious experiences.

I leave behind the smoke-filled cocktail party, the idle chatter, the superficiality of the crowd, and go off on my own. I inhale the fragrant, night air. I am under the stars by myself—alone—and yet not alone. Somehow I feel *with myself,* the self I really am, not the self I cover up by the chit-chat of the cocktail hour. In such a moment of solitude, I regain my sense of true self.

Celibate people as well as those in married life enjoy a unique experience of this sort. Married people may say that no matter how close they are to one another, there is always in their relationship what Adrian van Kaam calls a "celibate component"—an experience of being and needing to be alone. It is comparable to a moment by the shore when one sits on the soft sand gazing out over the waves and feels part of all that is.

The same may happen when I go on a vacation or a retreat. Away from the phone, from the demands of school, parish, family, or community, I relish my solitude. Times like these, when I am alone with myself, with those I love in deep communion, with my God in prayer, are true joy for the human person.

Notice, in loneliness, we speak about being *without*: without friends, without the possibility of communication, without hope for the future, seemingly without God. These experiences of being-without point to the difference between loneliness and solitude. Whenever we reflect on solitude, we use the word *with*: being alone with my thoughts at the shore or on retreat, with those I care for, with God.

Here is an interesting distinction. Loneliness is inevitably a "without" or separation experience, whereas solitude, in some paradoxical sense, is a "with" or communion experience. The positive value of solitude in the spiritual life is that it contributes to our communion with others and with God as well as to our participation in the world.

Solitude is thus a building stone for the inspirational side of the spiritual life, as is its companion, silence. Spiritual life can be seen as an intertwining unity of the inspirational and the incarnational.[1] Solitude and silence contribute to the inspirational side of the spiritual life and aid our quest for inner meaning. Such a life is open to the immediate meanings of the world as pointers to the transcendent.

We can never separate the inspirational side of the spiritual life from the incarnational. While solitude and silence facilitate the inspirational component, they also foster and deepen our possibility of participation in the world.

In Holy Scripture and the writings of the spiritual masters, we find sayings that point to the centrality of solitude in relation to both sides of the spiritual life. For example, in one of his *Sayings of Light and Love,* #76, St. John of the Cross asserts:

If you desire to discover peace and consolation for your soul and serve God truly, do not be content in this that you have left behind . . . but also leave all these other things and attend to the one thing alone, which brings all these with it, namely, holy solitude, together with prayer and spiritual and divine reading, and persevere there in forgetfulness of all things. For if these things are not incumbent upon yhou, you will be more pleasing to God in knowing how to guard and perfect yourself than by gaining all other things together, for what does it profit a man if he gains the whole world and suffers the loss of his soul? (Mt. 16:26)[2]

To understand these words of St. John, we have to recollect moments in our life when we felt overwhelmed by worries and deprived of inner peace. People and things were "incumbent" upon us. We lost ourselves in agitation and "inordinate attachment." We gained many things but failed to guard the tranquility of our soul. Now we need more than ever the holy solitude St. John mentions. This experience, complemented by prayer and spiritual reading, will unclutter our lives and allow the ultimate questions to surface: Who am I? Where is my life going? Answers to these questions often emerge in solitude. We find that our heart is dissatisfied whenever we forget God and cease to follow the inner directives of the Holy Spirit.

In his poem of love between the soul and God, *The Spiritual Canticle,* St. John has a haunting stanza that captures the essential meaning and necessity of solitude in the life of every person. He writes, in effect, that our deepest selves can find fulfillment only in God before whom we must one day stand alone.

She lived in solitude,
And now in solitude has built her nest;
And in solitude He guides her,
He alone, Who also bears
In solitude the wound of love.[3]

This stanza is about the soul-bride who finds and rejoices in Christ, her Beloved. She lives in solitude, detached from satisfactions and afflictions, from consolation and desolation—free as a solitary bird to rise above the things of the world and respond to the Holy Spirit in the depths of her heart. Her one desire is to do the will of God, to live for Him alone. Seeing the soul in such peaceful solitude, the Beloved Himself blesses her good will and guides her to the joys of divine intimacy. He finds her worthy to bear the wounds of love He Himself has borne for her sake. Through solitude, she gains inner peace and liberty of spirit.

The spiritual master sings here of the joy of being alone, not of its pain. As we ponder with Him the mystery of solitude, we see its fruits in the spiritual life. What might happen if we too build our nest in solitude? What if we really shake loose, for however short a duration, from all that unnecessarily clutters our lives? Dare we let our hearts leap out freely to meet the God who is with us?

If we take up the challenge offered by scripture and the spiritual masters, certain fruits of solitude become explicit. These are, first of all, the companionship of God; secondly, liberty of spirit; and thirdly, true knowledge of self.

In Chapter III, we reflected on the progression we find in Holy Scripture from the relationship of discipleship, to friendship, to sonship. The disciple listens to his Divine Master and resists the slogans of the crowd. The friend of Christ knows Him to be the only totally trustworthy lover whose main concern is his good. The son of God is drawn by Him to an ever increasing depth of intimacy that points to the first fruit of solitude—the graced companionship that exists between the soul and God.

It is interesting in this context to look again at the word "alone." It can be written thusly or rewritten as "all-one." Paradoxically, the deepest aloneness before God becomes an experience of all-oneness or at-oneness. Similarly, solitude can be seen as the ground of communion and graced companionship.

A lover of aloneness, the monk Thomas Merton, wrote a book entitled *Thoughts in Solitude*. He captures for us this mystery of aloneness and oneness—of being alone and at the same time of being God's companion. Then, through companionship with Him, we grow in loving nearness to our neighbor.

As soon as a man is fully disposed to be alone with God, he is alone with God no matter where he may be—in the

country, the monastery, the woods or the city. The lightning flashes from east to west, illuminating the whole
horizon and striking where it pleases and at the same instant the infinite liberty of God flashes in the depths of that
man's soul, and he is illumined. At that moment he sees
that though he seems to be in the middle of his journey, he
has already arrived at the end. For the life of grace on earth
is the beginning of the life of glory. Although he is a
traveller in time, he has opened his eyes, for a moment, in
eternity.[4]

If God grants us the grace of such a moment,
everything will be the same and yet everything will be
different. We experience ourselves as being touched
by the finger of God, of tasting, however briefly, the
fulfillment of His promise of lasting peace and joy.
Such moments, Merton would call, epiphanies of intimacy or companionship. Curiously enough, these
"lightning flashes" come in the midst of solitude.

A second fruit of solitude is liberty of spirit. This
freeing experience points to another mystery in Christianity—leaving all in order to gain all; losing our life
only to find it on a more profound level than any
amount of pleasure, power, or possession can provide; discovering a meaning that transcends gratification of immediate needs; casting our cares upon God
and trusting Him to take up the burden.

Spiritual masters assure us that this experience of
being with God, in which we renounce all that is not

God, is the key to liberty of spirit. We are freed interiorily by God from the blindness of egoism and sin. The detached soul lives the mystery of renunciation for the sake of liberation, as this description by St. John of the Cross shows:

> It makes little difference whether a bird is tied by a thin thread or by a cord. For even if tied by thread, the bird will be prevented from taking off just as surely as if it were tied by cord—that is, it will be impeded from flight as long as it does not break the thread. Admittedly the thread is easier to rend, but no matter how easily this may be done, the bird will not fly away without first doing so. This is the lot of a man who is attached to something; no matter how much virtue he has he will not reach the freedom of the divine union.[5]

If we are attached in an ultimate way to anything other than God, we cannot enjoy the freedom He wants for His children. This is the freedom to see clearly what He is doing in this world, to hear what He is asking of us, and to respond with a grateful heart. The liberated soul does not escape the dilemma-filled moments of life but enters into them from a faith horizon. She has the freedom to be flexible, to flow with God's will in the situation. Whatever holds us down—a small work or a great worry, a thin thread or a heavy chain—prevents the soul from soaring free and experiencing those moments when we are "care-less" because we are cared for by God. These may be wasteful moments, humanly speaking, but spiritually they are full of meaning. Such graced experiences transform us into living expressions of gratitude. They instill in us the wider vision that is a testimony that we are living the inspirational life.

Merton's *Thoughts in Solitude* confirm this gift of transformation and the grateful response it grants.

> The life of solitude therefore must be a continual communion and thanksgiving in which we behold by faith all that goes on in the depths of God, and lose our taste for any other life or any other spiritual food . . . We live in constant dependence upon this merciful kindness of the Father, and thus our whole life is a life of gratitude—a constant response to His help which comes to us at every moment . . . The solitary life is a life in which we cast our care upon the Lord and delight only in the help that comes from Him. Whatever He does is our joy. We reproduce His goodness in us by our gratitude.[6]

The liberty that leads to communion and thanksgiving attracts to itself, like a magnet attracts pieces of metal, other good fruits of the spiritual life. This liberty of spirit leads to the discovery of the third gift of solitude: true knowledge of self. Alone with God, we begin naturally to develop an inner attitude of presence to the self we most deeply are before him.

No matter where we happen to be, whether in a crowded bus or on a deserted beach, we may feel suddenly present to the limited yet free self that is uniquely ours and to the Divine Source of all life.

St. Teresa of Avila tells us that self-knowledge means to walk in the truth of who we are and of who God is calling us to become.[7] This attitude of presence must remain with us in times of peace as well as those of turmoil, for without it we may become lost in the crowd and forsake our life call. True knowledge of self tells us that there is always "something more" shimmering below the comfortable surface of things where we are in control. Where we leave off, the abyss begins. We sense how vulnerable we are. We depend on God for every breath. The person who lives a spiritual life does not cover up that mystery anymore. She tries to live in the reality of who she is: a child of God made in His image and likeness, a son called to union with the Father in expectation of the eternal homecoming He has promised will be ours.

Does this "other-wordly" attitude take us away from the "this-worldly" life, from the life of incarnation? Surely not. As we have seen, detachment frees us from the prison of partial truths and opens us to the whole and Holy. Out of solitude comes participation. Out of silence emerges the truest saying.

Persons who have experienced desert solitude discover these deeper self-dimensions. One such person is Nikos Kazantzakis, author of *Zorba the Greek.* He also wrote an autobiographical account of his life called *Report to Greco.* In a chapter of this book on "The Desert," he speaks thusly of his self-discovery.

> With the passage of days in this godly isolation, my heart grew calm. It seemed to fill with answers. I did not ask questions any more; I was certain. Everything—where we come from, where we are going, what our purpose is on earth—struck me as extremely sure and simple in this God-trodden isolation. Little by little my blood took on the godly rhythm. Matins, Divine Liturgy, vespers, psalmodies, the sun arising in the morning and setting in the evening, the constellations suspended like chandeliers each night over the monastery: all came and went, came and went in obedience to eternal laws, and drew the blood of man into the same placid rhythm. I saw the world as a tree, a gigantic poplar, and myself as a green leaf clinging to a branch with my slender stalk. When God's wind blew, I hopped and danced, together with the entire tree.[8]

His is a fragile, tender view of life, and yet one that is true to our experience. Kazantzakis' description touches us, for we too are like that little green leaf clinging to a branch. Everything about us is so vulnerable. We cling to the tree of life whose trunk is faith. We play our part in the divine symphony. We are not out of tune but in harmony with the entire universe. This harmony makes us happy to be alive and to be uniquely who we are.

Solitude is thus a first condition for the inward quest; a second is silence. A favorite biblical passage about silence comes from the Book of Wisdom (18: 14-15), which connects silence and the word.

> When peaceful silence compassed everything and the night in its swift course was half spent, down from heavens, from the royal throne leaped your all powerful Word; into the heart of a doomed land the fierce warrior leapt.

God broke the infinite silence of His eternal solitude and spoke one Word. That Word was His Son. St. John of the Cross has a saying that complements this message in his *Maxims on Love,* #21.

> The Father spoke one Word, which was His Son, and this Word he always speaks in eternal silence, and in silence must It be heard by the soul.'

In these texts we learn that the Word came forth from the silence and only in silence can we hear the Word. Hearing, in the sense of listening with our inner ears attuned to God's voice, presupposes two kinds of silence: attentive and deeply interior.

Attentive silence is not merely physical absence of noise or chatter. More than "shutting up," it involves an inner stilling. All of us experience that even though we might not talk, we are inwardly noisy. When our minds are overpopulated by images and ideas, it is difficult to make room for God. Inner noise abounds—a discord of confused thoughts, false expectations, and compulsive urges to contain the Infinite in my finite concepts. We set aside a twenty minute period for meditation and it takes us at least fifteen of those minutes to wind down and wind out of the pressures that occupy our minds. At least for the remaining five minutes, we clean out the mental clutter and enjoy in silence the Word that wants to be heard by our soul.

Ideally, inner stilling or attentive silence ought to increase my hearing of the voice of God and lead to deep interior silence. Merton calls this silence the mother of truth in which the mysteries of God are made known to man. It is the silence of Jesus' retreats in which He prayed to the Father before He took up His mission in the world. His silence must be ours if we want to be His disciples. Again, Merton's *Thoughts in Solitude* point to this truth.

When we have lived long enough alone with the reality around us, our veneration will learn how to bring forth a few good words about it from the silence which is the mother of Truth.

Words stand between silence and silence: between the silence of things and the silence of our own being. Between

75

the silence of the world and the silence of God. When we have really met and known the world in silence, words do not separate us from the world nor from other men, nor from God, nor from ourselves because we no longer trust entirely in language to contain reality.

Truth rises from the silence of being to the quiet, tremendous presence of the Word. Then, sinking again into silence, the truth of words bears us down into the silence of God.

Or rather God rises up out of the sea like a treasure in the waves, and when language recedes His brightness remains on the shores of our own being.[10]

Merton utters a fact we are inclined to overlook or repress in our communications-minded world. How interesting that in an age of encounter workshops and communication training there are less and less people able to talk to one another. In marriage encounter groups, for example, the main factor that emerges is that the couples cannot talk to one another. They are unable to communicate. Perhaps it is because we have trusted language too much; we have not admitted what Merton found out in silence, namely, that we can no longer trust entirely in language to contain reality.

There are some experiences that are too deep for words. When two people love one another, the most profound moments between them are wordless. They do not say anything and yet intense communication is going on. Such is the silent power of exchanges beyond words, where words would only prevent communication, where all that suffices is the gaze of respect and care.

Such non-verbal exchanges are mindful of what goes on between mother and child before the child is able to speak. By her touch, her look, her way of holding or nursing the baby, mother conveys a world of meaning. This rich experience of non-verbal communication is not unlike the wordless exchanges that go on between the soul and God. Here again language is not able to contain the reality of our union with the Divine Word, for this Word the Father always speaks in eternal silence, and in silence It must be heard by the soul. When language recedes, God's brightness remains on the shores of our being.

Attentive silence leading to that which is deeply interior increases the quality of our communication when it is time to speak. Speaking which emerges from the ground of silence in turn flows into action that is not impulsive or compulsive but reflective. Our response is in tune with God's inner direction of our life. Our words manifest wise personal decision; they do not merely mouth others' opinions.

A last point to be made about silence concerns the way in which it can be a witness to the Eternal. What impresses people long after they have forgotten our words is the quality of our presence. Though a spiritual master may say little, his silent presence speaks volumes. The power of Christ radiates through him and attracts new disciples. A fine example of this power is found in the story of the monk who learned the truths of faith from St. Anthony's silence.

> Three Fathers used to go and visit blessed Anthony every year and two of them used to discuss their thoughts and the salvation of their souls with him, but the third always remained silent and did not ask him anything. After a long time, Abba Anthony said to him, "You often come here to see me, but you never ask me anything," and the other replied, "It is enough for me to see you, Father."[11]

Solitude and silence are thus pillars of the inspirational life and the inward quest. They sustain in turn our outward quest to incarnate these values. Vitally, we are less agitated and more gracious; we accept our limits and are content to work within them. Functionally, we are less weighed down by nagging worries and more open to sharing with fellow solitaries the richness of Christian community life. Spiritually, we are less fearful of our faults and more reliant on God to be our strength in weakness.

Life is no longer a struggle for power, a goal to be possessed, an isolated moment of pleasure. Everyone and everything—myself included—finds the place in time allotted to us by the Eternal. Nourished and illumined by graced moments of being with God in solitude and silence, we are less tempted to abandon our commitments when obstacles emerge. We accept ambiguity, confusion, and difference of opinion as part of the human condition. We recognize anew that we are a community of solitary pilgrims in need of redemption.

We may thus conclude that solitude and silence, sustained by prayer and spiritual reading, mark neither the end of engagement nor the cessation of action; they are rather conditions for the possibility of true participation and communication. Solitude and silence bind us to our sacred source. Life becomes a rhythm of inspiration and incarnation, of solitude and sharing, of silence and saying. Inner vision and outer action unite as we remain open to the most profound mysteries made manifest in the simple goodness of everyday.[12]

PART TWO

FASHIONED BY THE WORD

VI.

"Mark well, then, the parable of the sower. The seed along the path is the man who hears the message about God's reign without understanding it. The evil one approaches him to steal away what was sown in his mind. The seed that fell on patches of rock is the man who hears the message and at first receives it with joy. But he has no roots, so he lasts only for a time. When some setback or persecution involving the message occurs, he soon falters. What was sown among briers is the man who hears the message, but then worldly anxiety and the lure of money choke it off. Such a one produces no yield. But what was sown on good soil is the man who hears the message and takes it in. He it is who bears a yield of a hundred- or sixty- or thirtyfold." (Mt. 13:13-23)

Seek in reading and you will find in meditation; knock in prayer and it will be opened to you in contemplation.

(St. John of the Cross, *Maxims on Love*)

VI

READINESS FOR SPIRITUAL READING

I know that your life like mine is busy,. but it is good to pause for a moment, if we can, and ask ourselves a question: When was the last time I felt really close to the Lord? Was it on the occasion of illness? When our forces wane, we often call on God to stay near and give us strength. Or perhaps we were present at the death of someone we loved; that person, we pray, lives on in God. Maybe we welcomed with joy the birth of a child or witnessed the marriage of a son or daughter. We thanked God for the blessings He bestowed and asked for His lasting benediction. Perhaps we felt the need for His presence in the midst of daily routine, pleading, "O God, give some meaning to my life." Was He near when, in a burst of gratitude, we got the position we were praying for?

In these and other common ways, we approach the Lord and feel our need to be with Him. We are with Him more intimately at Holy Mass; when we say our morning and evening prayers; at the time of mealtime grace or the practice of familiar devotions. Our Lord is with us always, but we may be more aware of Him when we listen to His word sounding through Holy Scripture and the writings of the spiritual masters.

These approaches to God represent one main side of the spiritual life that could be called *dispositive* or *facilitating*. We ready ourselves for the coming of the Lord into our lives. Like John the Baptist, we await the arrival of our Divine Master. In some measure we are the initiators of this readying action, though without His grace we could not approach Him at all. When we do spiritual reading, when we call out to the Lord in distress, when we express gratefulness for His gifts, we begin in some way a mysterious interaction. We are opening ourselves to a Presence that is in us and yet beyond us. We feel this presence often in the beauty of nature. Our senses like radar devices pick up the presence of the Lord in the wonder of creation. We open a space in our hearts in which the Divine Guest may manifest Himself in His own good time. Faith tells us that He dwells within, but to experience this intimacy, to feel ourselves 'oned' with Him, is a special gift of His Holy Spirit.

We are in Him and He is in us but, unfortunately, we too easily forget this miracle of intimacy. We ignore our Divine Visitor; we live in forgetfulness of His loving presence. The poet, T.S. Eliot, describes the problem we are facing in his poem, "Choruses from 'The Rock.'"

> The endless cycle of idea and action,
> Endless invention, endless experiment,
> Brings knowledge of motion, but not of stillness;
> Knowledge of speech, but not of silence;
> Knowledge of words, and ignorance of the Word.
> All our knowledge brings us nearer to our ignorance,
> All our ignorance brings us nearer to death.
> But nearness to death, no nearer to God.
> Where is the Life we have lost in living?
> Where is the wisdom we have lost in knowledge?
> Where is the knowledge we have lost in information?
> The cycles of Heaven in twenty centuries
> Bring us farther from God and nearer to the Dust.[1]

If the "dust" of forgetfulness has settled upon us, how can we regain the wisdom necessary to hear God's word? How can we, as a community of Christians, prepare our hearts anew for Christ's habitation? Surely many of us are trying to live a spiritual life, but we should not assume that merely because we are baptized, or because we belong to the Church or a religious community, that we live a life of presence to the Lord. No status by itself alone guarantees the life of intimacy God is calling us to. We have some preparation to do; we must open our hearts in receptivity to God's word.

Removing obstacles to spiritual reading, as well as creating conditions that facilitate it, are part of the preparation for God's advent in our life. In Holy

Scripture or in the text of spiritual masters inspired by scripture, God has spoken to His people; He has reached out and touched us through these words. On our side we must try to overcome any mood, thought, or feeling that lessens our sensitivity for the message of the Lord.

A first obstacle is lack of attention to the text due to distraction. Almost as soon as we pick up the text that busy train, which is our mind, begins to race. No sooner do we begin to dwell on the word than our mind jumps the track to what we did yesterday, what we have to do today, what we are going to do tomorrow. Plans, projects, reasons, excuses all buzz in: I'd better do this, not that; I have to be tops in my job, I can't waste time reading. As distractions rush in, we lose even the minimal attention due to sacred words. The solution is not to chase after these racing thoughts or to try willfully to repress them, for then we are in a double-bind—distracted by our distractions! The answer is firmly, but gently, to return to the text. This calm, steady return increases our attention and before long reduces distraction.

Another obstacle follows this one; reduction of the word to the narrowness of needs. When we read, are we merely pragmatists, looking for answers to problems? Do we expect the text to tell us how to solve a current difficulty? In a related manner, do we seek in reading a spiritual high? We may need a lift, but the Holy Spirit may or may not use the text to address us in this way. If we read only to feel uplifted, we may give up if nothing happens. Reducing the text to the narrowness of needs, we miss other messages it may reveal. A related problem has to do with our tendency to pick out the perfect text *for another person.* We decide this book is just what he needs, though we refuse to read it ourselves. We miss the docility of the true disciple we recommend so highly to others.

A third obstacle involves the lazy expectation that God will speak to us whether or not we set aside the time and space to listen to His word. We become overly confident *just because* we are living a decent life or *just because* we are students of spirituality. Such an expectation may signal a lack of humility, order and discipline—a disharmony that manifests itself in my refusal to set priorities. What comes first in my life, what second, what third? If my first love should be for God, why is it that I so often put my encounter with Him last on the list? Why is it that I give Him the dregs of my day—what's left over after everything else is done?

Here again, even though the Spirit is powerful, it is hard for Him to speak to my heart if I've fallen asleep on top of my book! Not to give Him optimal time is part of that lazy expectation that I don't have to do much to nourish my life of presence to Him. I expect deepening to take place automatically. I forget that the spiritual life is like a delicate plant that needs to be nourished lest it dwindle, dry up and possibly die, lest, as the poet says, "The cycles of Heaven in twenty centuries / Bring us farther from God and nearer to the Dust."

However, a reversal for the good may occur when we recognize that these obstacles can become aids in disguise. They should remind us that an "endless cycle of idea and action" blinds us to what God calls us to be. The hindrances we have been discussing—lack of attention, arrogant reduction, lazy expectation—can become helps if we listen to their opposites.

Instead of lack of attention, we can learn to wait upon the word. God does not conform to our time frame. We must be patient and live in an attitude of quiet expectation despite dryness and distraction. Attentive presence to his word strengthens our resolve to keep it.

This attitude of gentle expectancy helps us to overcome the second obstacle. Instead of reducing the word to meet my needs only, I dwell with it, even though it does not seem to solve immediate problems or answer current demands. Dwelling with the word in this way may reveal a far deeper insight into the will of God that transcends what I want at this moment. Sometimes the things that I need are only material—a better car or job, more popularity, increasing productivity, and the like. It is fine to bring these petitions before the Lord, provided we trust in the mysterious providential care of His divine plan for our lives. He may allow something to happen that we desperately do not want to undergo, like a change of professional status or the diminishment of the loving relationship one used to know in marriage. When such a thing happens, it tends to depress us; we feel unhappy. We seem incapable of reading the will of God in that situation; it is so contrary to what we feel is right for us. And yet, if we are people of faith, we can in time look back on such trials and see, in retrospect, that God knew what he was doing after all. We lost one position, but he placed us where we were more needed. The honeymoon ended, but our love deepened.

This attitude of trust is the opposite of demanding that God answer our needs as we desire. We have to dwell with the word and let it serve as a pointer with long range implications; its meaning goes beyond immediate action; it propels us into transcendent possibilities. We see unfolding the secret plan of God to draw us ever closer to Him.

Many spiritual masters have testified to the transforming power of waiting upon the word and dwelling with it. One of the most moving incidents recorded in the literature of spirituality involved a man who found in the word a clear revelation of God's will, though to obey would cost him much sacrifice and suffering. What happened to him in his friend's garden came after years of anguishing over what God was asking of him. Now, at the crucial turning point, Augustine writes:

RENEWED AT EACH AWAKENING

I flung myself down, how I do not know, under a certain fig tree, and gave free rein to my tears. The floods burst from my eyes, an acceptable sacrifice to you. Not indeed in these very words but to this effect I spoke many things to you: "And you, O Lord, how long? How long, O Lord, will you be angry forever? Remember not our past iniquities." For I felt that I was held by them, and I gasped forth these mournful words, "How long, how long? Tomorrow and tomorrow? Why not now? Why not in this very hour an end to my uncleanness?"

Such words I spoke, and with most bitter contrition I wept within my heart. And lo, I heard from a nearby house, a voice like that of a boy or a girl, I know not which, chanting and repeating over and over. "Take up and read. Take up and read." Instantly, with altered countenance, I began to think most intently whether children made use of any such chant in some kind of game, but I could not recall hearing it anywhere. I checked the flow of my tears and got up, for I interpreted this solely as a command given to me by God to open the book and read the first chapter I should come upon. For I had heard how Anthony had been admonished by a reading from the Gospel at which he chanced to be present as if the words read were addressed to him: "Go, sell what you have, and give to the poor, and you shall have treasure in heaven, and come, follow me," and that by such a portent he was immediately converted to you.

So I hurried back to the spot where Alypius was sitting, for I had put there the volume of the apostle when I got up and left him. I snatched it up, opened it, and read in silence the chapter on which my eyes first fell: "Not in rioting and drunkenness, not in chambering and impurities, not in strife and envying; but put you on the Lord Jesus Christ, and make not provision for the flesh in its concupiscences.'' No further wished I to read, nor was there need to do so. Instantly, in truth, at the end of this sentence, as if before a peaceful light streaming into my heart, all the dark shadows of doubt fled away.[2]

For you and I intimate contact with God through the power of his word may not happen in as dramatic a way, but any increase in openness helps to root out the last traces of arrogance and ready us for discipleship.

As to the third obstacle, instead of lazy expectation and lack of discipline, we become, as Augustine did, disciples of the word. We slow down; we step off the speeding train of activism and problem solving; we re-evaluate our priorities; we rediscover the purpose of life. The first fact facing us is that we only have so many years to live. Death stalks our days and tells us to make each one count. How limited we are. We can do only so much. We can help so many people and no more. We feel the weight of our limits when we stand before the mirror and see those wrinkles around our eyes and the first flock of gray hairs. We pluck a few out, a whole harvest replaces them!

The words of the scriptures and the masters are filled with reminders of human fallibility and the caution not to forget the Lord. Eliot speaks for the Lord when he says:

RENEWED AT EACH AWAKENING

O weariness of men who turn from God
To the grandeur of your mind and the glory of your action,
To arts and inventions and daring enterprises,
To schemes of human greatness thoroughly discredited,
Binding the earth and the water to your service,
Exploiting the seas and developing the mountains,
Dividing the stars into common and preferred,
Engaged in devising the perfect refrigerator,
Engaged in working out a rational morality,
Engaged in printing as many books as possible,
Plotting of happiness and flinging empty bottles,
Turning from your vacancy to fevered enthusiasm
For nation or race or what you call humanity;
Though you forget the way to the Temple,
There is one who remembers the way to your door;
Life you may evade, but Death you shall not.
You shall not deny the Stranger.[3]

As a finite being, I need to be present to Someone infinitely greater than I am. In these moments of vulnerability, I feel more strongly than ever the need for God's nearness. I do not want to "deny the Stranger." I want to become a true disciple of the word, treasuring each day as God's gift and not falling into "schemes of human greatness thoroughly discredited." If I do get lost in "vacancy" or "fevered enthusiasm," I beg God to let me find the way back to His door and, with a humble and contrite heart, to try again to live within the Temple. Why should I settle for anything less when God is calling me to so much more?

Thus far by slowing down and waiting upon the word, by trying to temper our arrogance and listen to God speaking in the depths of our heart, we've considered the action of readiness, of which we are the agent. We have suggested, with God's grace, how to overcome certain obstacles and create certain conditions that facilitate our openness to his word. Now what? The psalmist tells us: "Pause a while and know that I am God" (Ps. 46:11). Be still. Let go of all human problems and answers. Learn to be empty.

In other words, the scene shifts wholly to the side of God. From active striving we move to passive stilling, knowing that the gift of intimacy—of deepening in faith, hope and love—is just that, a gift, unmerited and undeserved. God is the agent of this contemplative action. Our efforts are good and necessary; God expects us to cooperate with his grace, for he usually grants these gifts according to the capacity of the soul to receive them. But in this receptive phase of spiritual deepening, what counts is less reason and more faith. We need to let go of our expectations of what God should do and simply believe that somehow, somewhere all things work together for our good if we surrender to him. Rather than rely on ecstatic feelings, we know that what matters most is the will to go on loving God in the dryness of desert places as well as in the consoling touches of his nearness.

Confirmation of this contemplative side of the life of presence is found in many sources. The masters speak reverently of this purely receptive moment and would concur with Thomas Merton's comment in his spiritual autobiography, *The Sign of Jonas* (July 25, 1948):

> . . . the desire to love God, the desire for perfect union with God means nothing at all and is without any value or merit whatever in the sight of God unless it is inspired and guided by grace and in conformity with God's will.
>
> There is a natural desire for contemplation which may never get to be explicit in most men, but it exists. All this is without merit or value. Our desire for God must come from God and be guided by His will before it means anything in the supernatural order.
>
> In all the aspects of life the supreme good which includes everything else is God's will. Without it, contemplation and virtue are nothing. The first movement in all prayer, together with faith in His presence, ought to be the desire to know His will and to abandon oneself entirely to all His dispositions and intentions for us.
>
> Without that, the desire of contemplation will only lead you to beat your head against a blank wall. But with it—peace.[4]

This peace that passes understanding is a gift the Lord alone can give. We can and must engage in the work of active striving, realizing that even our desire to dwell with the Lord more intimately and the strength to be faithful to this inspiration come from Him. We can be sure that if we are approaching God He is approaching us much more swiftly. If we are running after Him, He is running toward us. We may fall asleep but God does not doze. He wakes us so that we can hear and obey. With the prophet, we celebrate this graced relation of active striving and passive stilling and proclaim:

The Lord Yahweh has given me a disciple's tongue,
So that I may know how to reply to the wearied
    he provides me with speech
Each morning he wakes me to hear,
    to listen like a disciple
The Lord Yahweh has opened my ear.
For my part, I made no resistance
    neither did I turn away.

(Is. 50:4-6)

VII

"Anyone who loves me
will be true to my word,
and my Father will love him;
we will come to him
and make our dwelling place with him.
He who does not love me does not keep my words.
Yet the word you hear is not mine;
It comes from the Father who sent me.
(Jn. 14:23)

We rarely pray with the "mind" alone. Monastic medita-
tion, prayer, oratio, contemplation and reading involve the
whole man, and proceed from the "center" of man's be-
ing, his "heart" renewed in the Holy Spirit, totally sub-
missive to the grace of Christ. Monastic prayer begins not
so much with "considerations" as with a "return to the
heart," finding one's deepest center, awakening the pro-
found depths of our being in the presence of God who is the
source of our being and our life.

(Thomas Merton, *The Climate of Monastic Prayer*)

VII

LECTIO: A WAY TO ONENESS

Christianity is truly a religion of the word. In the Gospel of St. John we read:

> In the beginning was the Word:
> the Word was with God
> and the Word was God.

(Jn. 1:1-3)

When Jesus was led by the Spirit into the wilderness, he replied to Satan's taunting to turn stones into loaves: "Man does not live on bread alone, but on every word that comes from the mouth of God." (Mt. 4:4). Later he reminds us solemnly: "Heaven and earth will pass away, but my words will never pass away." (Mt. 24:35)

One of the ways in which we come to know this word is by spiritual reading. I bring to this art and discipline my whole self—my temperament, dispositions, and feelings, my unique social, cultural and educational background. For this reason the same text may mean different things to different people.

Certain factors in our contemporary world effect adversely our capacity to be and become spiritual readers. We seem generally restless. We have to be "in the know," to satisfy our curiosity, to keep up with the latest. We worship the problem solving mentality. Decision making seems to be impossible without setting up a committee or passing out a questionnaire. We need to be more clever, more well read, more knowledgeable than our neighbor. In our frantic search for easy answers, we worship time to the exclusion of eternity. Many substitute for true transcendence ecstatic feelings induced by drugs, alcohol, or dabbling in the occult. Some get lost in endless activity; work becomes their god; they feel worthwhile only when doing something. All of these symptoms of forgetfulness have an adverse effect on our possibility of doing spiritual reading.

Lectio divina requires not an outer ear stimulated by the media but an inner ear that listens to and is drawn in by words that convey perennial truth and beauty. It calls not for a problem solving mentality but an openness to mystery. We are to approach the text not as masters but as servants of the word. We must not always expect to feel something when we read. To do reading faithfully each day, whether or not we experience a "spiritual high," manifests the proper attitude. For, on the spirit level, I am to treat with equal calm, highs and lows, peaks and valleys, consolation and desolation. What counts day by day is living for God in ordinary events regardless of how I feel.

We may be living in a period of forgetfulness, but this crisis challenges us to purification. For ours is also an age of restoration in which we witness the effort of Christians and non-Christians, of religious and laity, to reclaim the values that make life worth living.

For example, we are less prone to treat our bodies as machines to be refueled. As a result, we are more than ever aware of the need for nutritious food, unpolluted water and air, clean neighborhoods and living conditions conducive to fostering human dignity. We are more vigilant toward technology because it has tampered so violently with these natural goods. We see again the need for discipline in our lives and the danger of placing everything at the disposal of man's technical intelligence. We are more inclined to question the meaning of our actions and only then to incarnate concretely our ideals. Discipline enables us to set conditions in daily life that facilitate spiritual growth such as prayer, liturgical participation, and spiritual reading.

We realize that to be alert and attentive to the word, we must be mindful of our basic metabolism. How does my body run? Am I a morning or an evening person? Can I pay attention on a full stomach or do I fall asleep? As a sensing body, I realize that there is an implicit interaction between me and the space I inhabit. What location is most conducive for my spiritual reading? Cafeteria or chapel, public bench or private room? Am I able to schedule my day in such a way that I set aside regular times for spiritual reading? According to my state of life (clerical, religious, lay) can I wisely select which books to read, at least Holy Scripture and some masters of the spiritual life? Do I know the difference between reading for information and formative reading? The way I read the psalms, for instance, is necessarily different from the way I approach the daily papers. Spiritual reading is less devouring and more dwelling, less inclined to watch the clock and more willing to let things happen in God's time, less seeking for answers and more inclined to place oneself in question.

I must not violate the text by forcing it to fit into my narrow categories of thought. My reading mood ought to be gentle and easy going, not vehement or agitated. If I prejudge what the text is going to mean, I may violate its possibility to address me personally. I do not allow the text to touch my life but decide in advance what it will or will not say. My eye becomes expert at fault finding. Worst of all I raise all kinds of subtle defenses to resist the words of the spiritual master that are meant to be transforming.

For example, I dismiss the text as old-fashioned because I convince myself that anything over ten years old is obsolete. I forget that the great masters of the spiritual life communicate transtemporal truths as striking in our age as any other. Or I develop the clever ploy of aesthetic resistance. I acknowledge how beautiful this passage is but at the same time I refuse to get involved in the implications of its meaning. I treat the text as an ancient artifact to be admired rather than a current message to be assimilated.

When I do spiritual reading, I let go of my defenses and place myself before the text as the needy pilgrim I am. I welcome the guidance the sacred word is able to give. This mood of discipleship marks the spiritual reader who, above all, respects the word, especially the revealed words of Jesus in the Gospels.

Each word of Jesus carries a wealth of wisdom I reverence and respect. My respectful presence to the word carries me into the heart of Jesus' message of salvation. He is the eternal self-expression of the Father. Through the finite vehicle of these inspired words, I meet the Infinite Master whose message leads me to eternal life.

Care for the Divine Word in words places me on the road toward my eternal homeland. In sacred words I meet the Word who is behind all words. Through the art and discipline of spiritual reading, I begin to make His words my own; I let myself be led into their healing light and step by step I take them to heart.

In the life of the spirit there are many ways to come nearer to Jesus, the Word made flesh who hides in my heart. There are ways of mortification and prayer, of sacrifice and liturgical celebration, of asceticism and mystical union. There is also the way of *lectio divina,* recommended by spiritual masters from the beginnings of monasticism to the present age—one that needs to be restored in our time by lay people, priests and religious.

Ours is a God who has spoken to His people. His Word dwells among us and calls us to union with Father, Son and Holy Spirit. *Lectio* is a way to oneness. It is no guarantee, for union with the Holy Trinity is a gift of grace, but at least we can prepare ourselves to receive this gift should God choose to grant it.

Spiritual reading in its fullest sense is a participation in the eternal. It is an act of worship, praise, thanksgiving. *Worship* of the Divine for having revealed Himself to us. *Praise* of Him as He is and not as we would have Him be. *Thanksgiving* for His allowing to emerge in our midst the words of spiritual masters who are God's messengers, ordained by Him to communicate wisdom that might otherwise remain undisclosed. By reading their words, more importantly, by living them in daily life, we do our part to keep this sacred dialogue alive. For if ours is a God who has spoken to His people, He is also a God who needs to be heard, if only by a handful of His chosen.

VIII

He summoned the crowd with his disciplines and said to them: "If a man wishes to come after me, he must deny his very self, take up his cross, and follow in my steps." (Mk. 8:34)

Like the Jews in Egypt we have spent all our lives as slaves; we are not yet in our souls, in our wills, in our whole selves, real free men: left to our own powers we may fall into temptation. And these words, 'Lead us not into temptation'—submit us not to the severe test—must remind us of the forty years the Jews spent crossing the short expanse of territory between the land of Egypt and the promised land. They took so long because whenever they turned away from God, their path turned away from the promised land. The only way in which we can reach the promised land is to follow in the steps of the Lord. Whenever our heart turns back to the land of Egypt, we retrace our steps, we go astray. We have all been set free by the mercy of God, we are all on our way, but who will say that he does not retrace his steps constantly, or turn from the right path? 'Lead us not into temptation,' let us not fall back into our state of slavery.

(Anthony Bloom, *Living Prayer*)

VIII

MOVING FROM MASTERY TO DISCIPLESHIP

I once met a parish priest whose reputation for apostolic activity was legendary. Father Dominic did everything from cooking to hearing confessions, from maintenance work to pastoral counseling. He told me when I met him that his ulcers were acting up. Was he out of touch with the spiritual motivation of his service? Was it time to take stock of his life? Could he listen to what God was asking of him in the depths of his heart?

Gradually, he began to see what was at the base of his problem. In his commitment to care for others as pastor, teacher and director of souls, he had lost the balance between "inside and outside." He was fast becoming a purely external person. In his desire to work actively for the good of others, he had forgotten his own inner feelings. He was so proud of caring for them that he repressed his own need to be cared for. He was so intent on being useful that he took less and less time simply to be before God in prayer.

He came to discover this lack of an inner life in a variety of ways. For one thing, he learned to read certain vital signs. He took a good look in the mirror at his tired, exhausted body. "Nick," he said, "you've become a clerical wreck!'' Needed relaxation was willfully forsaken under the pressure of morning, afternoon and evening appointments. In trying to play God for his faithful flock, he had forgotten to assess his limits. He had kept on giving without taking time off to be restored. Now he had to pay the price for such neglect. The fatigue lines showed in his face. Whenever he wanted to slow down, do some reading, go to a film, have coffee with a friend, a little ''ego button'' kept pushing, pushing—compelling him to live under constant pressure.

In neglecting to care for himself, he saw that he had neglected an essential component of the spiritual life, namely, gentle presence to the limited person he was. He had been harsh on himself, feeling as if he had to carry the whole of God's kingdom on his shoulders. Not surprisingly, he became a hazard to the people he was caring for. Instead of meeting a gentle, Christ-like man, radiating the good news of Jesus' peace and joy, they beheld a nervous, irritable person, who alternated between outright anger and repressed agitation.

This pattern of over-exertion and ego control persisted for several months. Fortunately, a good friend convinced him that he should go for some spiritual direction and begin to deal with this difficulty. Gradually he could see that, among other problems, he definitely had what his director called an ''Atlas-complex." He felt as if the weight of the world—the whole school, the whole country, the whole church—was on his back. A symptom of this complex showed up in his inability to really go on vacation. Even when he was away, he would be living mentally in the past (that desk piled high with work) or imaginatively in the future (what I have to do as soon as I return home). He really could not relax. He would even overexert himself in play, trying to get in as much golf as he could, as much sun, as much touring as possible. He would fall into his motel bed in the exact exhausted state he was in when he fell into bed at home.

It was hard for Father Dominic to let go and flow with the vacation mood that is so supportive of the spiritual life. He and his spiritual director discussed the value of surrendering to God and remembering that he cares for us in a personal way. "The God who asks me to serve Him loves me," Dominic thought. "He wants to be my strength and sustaining ground. He does not expect me to do all this work alone; He does expect me to remember that without Him I can do nothing." Father was convinced of the necessity to experience God's care so he could inwardly renew his ministry and teaching career.

One week during the summer he had an extraordinary experience that brought home these three factors: caring for others, caring for himself, and being cared for by God. He decided to take a real vacation, this time on the New England shore. Packing his car, he felt the same nervous tension creeping up, but at least he could keep in touch with what was happening and not try to cover it up with his old tactic of being extra busy. "Thank God," he thought, "this period of reflection has done some good." Driving to his destination, he allowed his mind to drift back to the previous two months of the summer.

Sure enough, he had fallen into his old pattern. In addition to his regular duties, he had volunteered for several extra jobs, enjoying the expected laudatory remarks about what a caring fellow he was. He tried to cover up the tension on more than one occasion, but the vital signs came back to warn him of the danger he was in: a nervous stomach, indigestion, trembling hands, sweaty temples. Body stiffness, and a certain rigidity typical of the Atlas-complex, set in. A far cry from the relaxed, gracious, flexible presence he wanted to be. That little "ego button" with its computer brain was tapping out orders again. He'd have to do more. He'd have to move faster. He'd have to . . . but wait . . . fortunately, he was able to stop and take a deep breath and say, "Hold it. There you go again, Falling into the same trap. Feel how tense you are. It's written in your body." He had learned by now to pay attention to the vital signs that something was wrong. Instead of radiating the peace and joy of the children of God, he looked in the mirror and saw his facial muscles tensing up; he looked at his hands and felt his fists clenching. That's when he decided to take a week off and pay attention to the self he typically refused to take care of.

"Enough backtracking," he mused. "You've been on the road for an hour and you haven't even seen the beautiful scenery. Remember how important it is to be here . . . to be now . . . What a magnificent drive this is!"

A few days later, sitting on the beach, this experience happened. His tense body had started to relax. All the tasks done and undone had receded into the background. He was practicing the art of being in the present, in the here and now, and enjoying it immensely. He preached a few good homilies. He answered pastoral calls in the afternoon and evening. He was faithful to his religious duties. But what were all those accomplishments compared to the care God had shown for this world? A feeling unlike anything he had ever felt before slowly began to invade him. Afterwards he called it a religious experience, the first in his life, though he had been ordained for years.

It was hard to put into words the breathless wonder that grasped him. He suddenly opened up to all that was out there and beheld it with new eyes. His eyes were like those with which a child sees his first flower or beholds the face of his mother. Of course, he had seen the same sights before and yet he had never really beheld their transcendent beauty. The ocean, the sun, the sand, the waves, his own body—all became an overwhelming expression of God's care. This earth, this cosmos, this little man sitting on the beach—all ordered so finely, all fitting together, all held, sustained, carried, created by an infinitely Caring Hand. What happened to him defied definition. It was a personal experience of God as the caring Father of creation and of himself as being caught up in his creatureliness by this Loving Someone. This overworked, unworthy, limited person was really loved. The hardest part of the experience to describe was the sense of an inner voice saying, "You are my child, I care for you. I sustain you. I hold you. I forgive you." Never would he forget those words nor the impact of what he had experienced.

A little sand crab scurried under his feet. He reached out and held it for a moment. It was as fragile, vulnerable, and dependent as he. If he could care for the crab, how much more must God care for him? The feeling of wonder faded, only to be replaced by a feeling of overwhelming tenderness. All the tension drained off and flowed into the softly undulating waves. The unspeakable order of everything in the universe assured him of the mystery of life and of his being a tiny but precious part of this holy composition.

The experience probably lasted only a few minutes but for him it was a "watershed moment." After that, things began to fall into place. He smiled to himself and pondered if the "Rock of Gibraltar," as his fellow priests called him, was becoming a romantic. Perhaps he needed a little poetry in his life. He had thought he could be happy living on the surface, but now that he had tasted the depth dimension, he wanted more.

Being "Johnny-Do-Good" gave him a lot of gratification but didn't allow much time for spiritual growth. Having all the answers did not mean that he was becoming a person in whom his parishioners could behold Christ. He had to begin to ask some questions of ultimate concern and not jump to his own conclusions. "Maybe this is what it means to care for yourself," he thought. "It's not a dramatic occurrence but a matter of keeping in touch with the inner person. Once I'm with Christ I know I can go on caring for others, only I'll be free of the Atlas-complex. I'll do my limited best and leave the rest up to the Lord."

Being cared for by God and becoming a caring presence for self thus precede genuine care for others. The first step calls for faith—the faith that God loves me in a personal way with all my limits and possibilities. He expects me to try to do my best and cautions against perfectionism. The second step implies gentleness—so different from the harsh judgmental response to my failings or the inhuman effort to be in control of every detail. Gentleness toward self shows up when I pay attention to my tiredness; when I work as well as I can but slow down as soon as I perceive the body's signals of overwork; when I cease pretending that I'm all powerful and seek help. The third step finds expression in compassion and fraternal charity. Because I have learned to suffer with myself, I can suffer with others. Because I can admit my own need to be cared for, I can go out to others and respond to their manifold needs—cautious to stay within the limits of my capacity and not trying to play God.

The vacation was over. The week came to an end but the person who drove back to the city was different. Father Dominic looked the same, though some of the fatigue lines had faded and he felt much more relaxed; inside he was different. An inner transformation of attitude had taken place and the lessons of the past year had begun to be personalized. He had no illusions about his limits—they would still be there. But now he could be more accepting of them. Whenever the Atlas-complex threatened to take over, he could turn back in memory to the shore experience of the Divine touching him and try to let go. He felt at least that he could be more in tune with who he was and possibly more in tune with what others wanted deep down without knowing it. They, too, must be searching for themselves and hungry to meet the God who cared.

One concrete fruit of this self insight was already evident. He noticed that his homilies were becoming more down to earth. Before, his nervousness and desire for perfection had caused him to talk far above the people; he was always trying to impress them with his knowledge of theology, or his concern for current social issues, but seldom did he sense in their response that he was really touching their lives. Either he would talk above them or talk down to them in a kind of clerical condescension. Now he felt more able to identify with his parishioners. He wanted to meet them not as an expert with all the answers but as a servant who, like them, was in search of the Divine Master. Where before he could talk *to* a person, now he could be *with* him. He could feel what he was feeling (sadness, joy, sorrow, celebration) and at the same time not be overwhelmed by these feelings.

Most of all he could open himself to God in prayer and offer himself as a channel through which Christ could work to reach others. He realized that he was not the source of God's power but only its pathway. His capacity to bring the Word to others would only be as worthwhile as the depth of his own presence to the Lord. In the simplest terms, he knew that he could not give what he himself did not live. The Word would remain mere definition or abstraction unless he filled it with a personal presence—a quality of being that speaks more clearly than any tricks or technique one can invent to get the message across.

The Divine Word became a personal word for him and others could perceive what was happening. A smile, a sudden meeting of understanding eyes, a quick squeeze of the hand—in small ways his flock expressed their appreciation and added to his already rich experience a fourth factor—being cared for by others.

I've narrated this experience to place us in touch with our own experience as caring people and also because we are in danger of losing touch with ourselves as cared for by others and by God. Perhaps sharing in the experience of Father Dominic can help us to catch ourselves before we forget the deepest meaning of our Christian commitment: to be carriers of Christ's personal care for souls. He wants to be present to others through us. If the other only sees me with my cleverness and control, I may have to answer to the Lord for breeding in the faithful entrusted to my care a whole set of wrong attitudes. Instead of humility, I may teach them arrogance; instead of inner silence, loving the sound of their own voice; instead of selfless giving, selfish gain; instead of remembering God and relying on his grace, making vain attempts at self redemption.

As we have seen, developing religious attitudes calls for creating certain conditions, inwardly and outwardly, that dispose us more fully to receive God's outpouring of grace. For instance, an inner attitude of openness to God's call in each life situation fosters spiritual emergence. Outwardly, an atmosphere of quiet, or the setting aside of silent periods for reflection and spiritual reading, aid religious deepening. The importance of spiritual reading has long been recognized by all branches of Christianity, as we find our common basis in God's revealed word. We respect the word and desire to approach it as disciples. To live as a disciple is to be a listener to the Divine Word. It is to know that despite our limits as creatures, we are called to partake of the intimacy shared by the Divine Persons. As disciples, we can be a channel through which others come to know the Lord.

Contrary to the mode of discipleship is that of mastery. On the level of day to day functioning, mastery is appropriate. At times I need to fight for my rights, defend my position, adapt to the demands of changing times, meet my commitments. The difficulty is that this mode can take over, even when a more docile approach is called for. To solve a problem I need a mentality of mastery, but spiritual life is a mystery. It addresses itelf to perennial truths that teach of love and openness to the depth dimension of reality.

To temper the mode of mastery, the disciple may dwell upon sacred texts, asking God for the grace to make their message his own. He realizes that one reading can never exhaust the richness of the word, so he gladly turns to it again and again to foster his conversion as a worthy messenger of the Lord. He seeks in the word enduring values—truths that transcend the time bound vicissitudes of culture and tap into the wellspring of lasting wisdom.[1] Amidst the turmoil of change, he opts to safeguard Christ's eternal truth. Rather than being caught in the immediacy of things, he tries to tune into the transcendent movement of the Spirit.

The mode of mastery is fine for the professional sphere, but it is not enough for the spiritual pilgrim. The priest whose story we told found that out and each of us must do the same. Father Dominic learned to listen to himself and in so doing became a better listener to God. He dared to step off the treadmill of mere functionality and ask himself what happened to the caring pastor he wanted to be. He faced the fact that his presence was not appealing to others despite the exhaustion he felt in the wake of apostolic zeal. Luckily he heeded the inner signals that told him mastery had taken over. He heard the voice of his Divine Master and once again vowed to be His disciple. As arrogant doing gave way to gentle being, he discovered a new capacity to care. He knows it will take a lifetime to grow beyond the obstacles to discipleship, but at least he is trying—and that's what counts in God's eyes, for, in the words of the poet:

> . . . what there is to
> conquer
> By strength and submission, has already been discovered
> Once or twice, or several times, by men whom one cannot
> hope

RENEWED AT EACH AWAKENING

To emulate—but there is no competition—
There is only the fight to recover what has been lost
And found and lost again and again; and now, under
    conditions
That seem unpropitious. But perhaps neither gain nor loss.
For us, there is only the trying. The rest is not our
    business.[2]

IX

"If you live in me,
and my words stay part of you,
you may ask what you will—
it will be done for you.
My Father has been glorified
in your bearing much fruit
and becoming my disciples."

(Jn. 15:7-8)

You know that God is everywhere; and this is a great truth, for, of course, wherever the king is, or so they say, the court is too: that is to say, wherever God is, there is Heaven. No doubt you can believe that, in any place where His Majesty is, there is fulness of glory. Remember how Saint Augustine tells us about his seeking God in many places and eventually finding Him within himself. Do you suppose it is of little importance that a soul which is often distracted should come to understand this truth and to find that, in order to speak to its Eternal Father and to take its delight in Him, it has no need to go to Heaven or to speak in a loud voice? However quietly we speak, He is so near that He will hear us: we need no wings to go in search of Him but have only to find a place where we can be alone and look upon Him present within us. Nor need we feel strange in the presence of so kind a Guest; we must talk to Him very humbly, as we should to our father, ask Him for things as we should ask a father, tell Him our troubles, beg Him to put them right, and yet realize that we are not worthy to be called His children.

(St. Teresa of Avila, *The Way of Perfection*)

IX

SPIRITUAL FORMATION OF THE DISCIPLE

In discussing the spiritual formation of the disciple, we are interested in the inner and outer conditions that foster or hinder his personal-spiritual unfolding in Christ. Noting the resurgence of interest in the life of the spirit typical of today's youth makes us aware of the vital role the Christian witness has to play in that renewal. He has to go beyond mere rational "shoulds" or wishful "could be's" to really identify experientially with the historical situation in which the Lord is speaking. The Divine Master is inviting us to spread the fruits of His Spirit that will revolutionize the world in the deepest sense.

If we are to remember who we most deeply are in God and to retain the gift of peace He wants to instill in our hearts, we need "stepping-aside" moments—times in which to reflect again on the enduring truths and values of the Christian life.

A poem by Walt Whitman illustrates vividly this necessity for stepping-aside. It also sets the tone for our consideration of the disciple's personal appropriation of the word through spiritual reading. Whitman describes an experience of being at a conference of astronomers who are intent on looking at the stars, measuring and identifying them. The poet, in contrast to this calculating audience, is a man of spiritual sensitivity. He pauses, therefore, to reflect on his own feelings.

> When I heard the learn'd astronomer,
> When the proofs, the figures, were ranged in columns
>   before me,
> When I was shown the charts and diagrams, to add, divide
>   and measure them,
> When I sitting heard the astronomer where he lectured
>   with much applause in the lecture room,
> How soon unaccountable I became, tired and sick,
> Till rising and gliding out I wander'd off by myself,
> In the mystical moist night-air, and from time to time,
> Look'd up in perfect silence at the stars.[1]

This man wants to keep alive the child in him; he does not want charts and diagrams to take him away from the human experience of the stars and the wonder they evoke.

The Lord Jesus, our Divine Master, told us that the one thing we must not lose is the childlike quality of wonder, trust, and care characteristic of those who enter His kingdom.

> People were bringing their little children to him to have him touch them, but the disciples were scolding them for this. Jesus became indignant when he noticed it and said to them: "Let the children come to me and do not hinder them. It is to such as these that the kingdom of God belongs. I assure you that whoever does not accept the reign of God like a little child shall not take part in it. Then he embraced them and blessed them, placing his hands on them. (Mk. 10:13-19)

Youngsters are often a delight to behold with their rosy cheeks, flying pigtails, trim school frocks. Their lilting voices fill the air as they share with one another the day's adventures. What a wonderfully alive spirit they enjoy! So different from the business set weighed down by the world and carrying their "Atlas-complexes" in their briefcases. One ponders, while comparing the bright-eyed boy and the busy executive, "What ever happened to the child in him? What took away that glow? Was it the takeover of monetary values? The loss of humility and humor? Was it education? Did educators unwittingly dampen the spirit of creativity? Can wonder be regained or is it forever repressed by the merely functional mode?"

What the Lord Jesus wants to keep alive in us is not the three year old at the "no" stage or the adolescent rebelling against all human limits, but the spirit self. Because I am spirit, I can attain a "natural high" by gazing at the stars. Because I am openness to the beyond, I can unabashedly worship their Source.

What the Lord Jesus never wants us to lose is the spirit of joy and simplicity. Then we shall inherit his kingdom and, already on earth, savor its fruits of joy, gentleness, and peace.

Being a child of God does not mean giving up our passionate commitments or suppressing our genuine desire to do something in this world. The invitation to childlikeness is not an excuse for passivity but a challenge to return to Christ's word and abide in its truth. Amidst the confusion of life, we can approach Him in trust. Because the light of His truth enables us to reset our priorities in the spiritual realm, we can move back into the world and respond to the hunger for God our fellow men feel.

Professional interpreters of the word—priests, ministers, religious teachers—must listen with especially keen attention to Jesus' teaching about their task.

Just then the disciples came up to Jesus with the question "Who is of greatest importance in the kingdom of God?" He called a little child over and stood him in their midst and said: "I assure you, unless you change and become like little children, you will not enter the kingdom of God. Whoever makes himself lowly, becoming like this child, is of greatest importance in that heavenly reign. Whoever welcomes one such child for my sake welcomes me. On the other hand, it would be better for anyone who leads astray one of these little ones who believe in me, to be drowned by a millstone around his neck, in the depths of the sea. . . .

See that you never despise one of these little ones. I assure
you, the angels in heaven constantly behold my heavenly
Father's face . . . it is not part of your heavenly Father's
plan that a single one of these little ones shall ever come to
grief . . .'' (Mt. 18: 1-14)

When, as disciples, we listen to this word of warning,
we cannot help but feel the pangs of compunction. In
our personal history, all of us can point to instances
where we led another astray. That flare up of anger,
that impatient look in response to a student's
mistake, that unkind remark overheard in the
hall—any instance like this could have blocked
Christ's possibility to reach another through me. That
is why the disciple has as a main responsibility to
renew his inner life before God. One aid to this
renewal is spiritual reading.

When we do spiritual reading, there are four experiences, related to one another, that foster our personal in-touchness with sacred words. These are the
experience of resonance; the experience of resistance;
the personally reflective pause; and the possible formation or reformation of lasting spiritual attitudes.

Resonance. We may be reading a passage from
scripture, the text of a poet, or the writings of a
spiritual master in the slowed down manner that
distinguishes spiritual from mere informational
reading. We have created facilitating outer conditions
for inner listening by setting aside time and space for

this practice. As we read along, slowly and reflective-
ly, a word may suddenly "leap from the page." It
touches us personally. We may not know exactly why
we are resonating with the word but that it has touched us is undeniable.

This "aha" experience may be evidence that the
Holy Spirit has used the vehicle of the written word to
communicate to us a message of importance for our
spiritual lives. It is helpful to put a check mark beside
that message or underline it because we may want to
come back to it later and further explore what really
resonated for us. Was it the beauty of the text that
satisfied our aesthetic sense? Was it a word that
tapped into a private exchange between God and me?
Did the text offer consolation at a time of my life
when I was experiencing spiritual dryness?

The resonating moment can happen for any
number of reasons. The important thing is to try later
to reflect upon it. As we shall see in a moment, this
reflection can be aided by the keeping of a spiritual
reading notebook.

Resistance. Side by side with "aha" moments in
spiritual reading can come moments of resistance. We
do not feel in agreement with the text nor do we like
its message. We feel negative about or indifferent to
what we are reading. It is as helpful to identify texts
that "turn us off" as it is to mark those that "turn us
on." Resistance tells us something about ourselves as
much as resonance. These negative responses ought

also to be taken up in the third stage of the personally reflective pause. Interestingly, we often learn more about where we are spiritually by getting in touch with our resistances than by paying attention only to the positive feelings. "Bad vibrations" set off by the encounter of reader and text can be occasions for gaining insight as much as "good vibrations," if not more so.

Personally Reflective Pause. Following this first and second phase of spontaneously marking off points of resonance and resistance, we move into the third phase of the personally reflective pause. As spiritual readers, our goal is not merely to take in information but to move toward personal appropriation. During this pause period, we try to discover the reasons for our resonance or resistance. We dialogue with both experiences. An aid to this dialogue can be the spiritual reading notebook in which we record the results of our reflection.

For instance, a passage of scripture may resonate with meaning for me. The reason for this may have something to do with my here and now situation. Perhaps hearing Jesus rebuke those who led the children astray causes me to admit that I've grown more arrogant in my teaching career. That arrogance breeds anger and impatience with those who do not see my point. I am inclined to dismiss all who disagree with me as fools. Recording this honest, self-searching reflection in a notebook can help me to further work this problem through; it can also remind me of my need to keep the Lord's word before me continually, lest I substitute for His counsel my own one-sided conclusions. Writing out a brief reflection can lead me to turn to Him in prayer and ask for the grace I need to transform my life.

The same approach can help me to deal with my resistances. When a word really irritates me, I need to find out why? Is it because the text is too archaic? Is its message too time bound to say anything to me today? Or am I resisting because the text has touched too close to the truth of my life? I may call the language archaic and attempt to dismiss the text for that reason alone, but the fact that it disturbed me so much may lead me to search for another reason. Beneath this old fashioned language may be a message of timeless meaning for the sincere seeker. Again I may resist Jesus' words about the children by calling them sentimental, poetic, lacking in psychological astuteness, too simple to be taken seriously. But the fact that these words irritated me may be a pointer to the truth they are touching—a truth that hurts me because I know deep down how far I've departed from this Gospel ideal.

Resistance may also happen because I fear the implications of the text's message. If I take the word seriously, it may mean that I have some soul searching to do—and that can be painful. I have to think about changing my ways before it is too late;

perhaps I find something in me of the pharisee Jesus condemned.

Tracing out my resistance in a spiritual reading notebook can also help me to identify certain traits that are generally detrimental to spiritual reading. We place these under the heading of "academic games." These games diminish the mode of discipleship and lessen greatly the possibility of coming to self-knowledge through spiritual reading. One of these games is "one-upmanship." I am secretly waiting for the writer to say something that will give me a chance to say something more clever. Another game is that of "negative identity." I am paying less attention to what the writer is saying and more attention to what he is *not* saying. I am like the person who never sees the artist's work as a whole because he is so intent on closely scrutinizing its flaws. Lastly, there's the problem of "name-dropping." I am likely to dismiss the text as irrelevant because the writer while quoting X seems to know nothing about Y. In my eyes anyone who is anyone should know about him!

These games, which may be difficult to avoid in the competitive sphere of professional accomplishment, diminish greatly the chances of doing spiritual reading. There my approach is not so much to find fault with the master as to let him find fault with me. I am not out to lead; I desire to be led. I do not want initially to go counter to the text; I want to encounter it as friend to friend, walking side by side to the same sacred goal. I want to wait upon the word in a gentle way, tempering all traces of academic arrogance.

A related resistance can happen in the aesthetic realm. The beauty of the text can be an occasion for resonance, but it can also conceal a subtle resistance. In the latter case, I acknowledge the loveliness of the text, as a connoisseur would relish a beautiful work of art, but I maintain a careful detachment from its message. I admire the text as an ancient artifact, helpful for historical comprehension, but not able to touch me deeply. I enjoy having this book on my shelf to impress my friends, but I resist getting into the heart of its message for me.

For instance, we can admire the poetic excellence of the following passage from T.S. Eliot's *Four Quartets,* but do we dare meditate upon its demands for personal-spiritual deepening?

                    You say I am repeating
Something I have said before. I shall say it again.
Shall I say it again? In order to arrive there,
To arrive where you are, to get from where you are not,
    You must go by a way wherein there is no ecstasy.
In order to arrive at what you do not know
    You must go by a way which is the way of ignorance.
In order to possess what you do not possess
    You must go by the way of dispossession.
In order to arrive at what you are not
    You must go through the way in which you are not.
And what you do not know is the only thing you know

And what you own is what you do not own
And where you are is where you are not.[2]

This is a text that has many levels of meaning. Some
we may resonate with; others we may resist. But clearly the poet is repeating the traditional wisdom of the
spiritual life, his inspiration for this passage being
Book I, Chapter 13 of *The Ascent of Mount Carmel*
by St. John of the Cross. Eliot is speaking about the
formation of lasting spiritual attitudes: living in
everydayness (vs. ecstasy) in imitation of the Lord;
living within the mystery of all things that resists sub-
jugation by our analytical intelligence (the way of ig-
norance); living in poverty of spirit versus the greed
of possessiveness. The poet helps us to understand
that spiritual "highs" may come—but not usually.
The life of the spirit happens amidst the routines of
everyday life. I can only fill these routines with meaning, and not give way to negativity and apathy, to the
degree that I identify with the hidden holiness that
resides in every person, event, and thing on this earth
because the Incarnate Word walked upon it.

Formation of Lasting Life Attitudes. While some
of us may be granted the grace of mystical experience,
most of us have to find meaning not on mountain
tops but in kitchen, classroom, research lab or
library. To find this meaning requires that the
wisdom gained through spiritual reading remain not

"out there," as an interesting piece of information, but "in here" as the flesh and bones of my life with the Lord. My aim must be to form and reform myself in the light of lasting spiritual values. I do so by following the path of spiritual repetition.

Difference from the automatic repetition of, say, learning to tie a shoe, spiritual repetition is an exercise of spiraling deeper and deeper into the treasure of meaning residing in sacred texts. Reading becomes a gathering place for the essential components of my personal-spiritual life, such as self-knowledge, wonder, humility, prayer, and praise. These attitudes are the "matter" of the spiritual life to which I give "form" in my day-to-day existence.

When I find these attitudes referred to again and again by spiritual writers, I feel reinforced in my own quest for intimacy with the Divine. Others have trod upon this path before me; they can teach me something about the pitfalls to avoid and the right roads to follow. We know something about these ways through our upbringing in the family and through our membership in the Church, but still we are inclined to forget them. We miss many opportunities for personalization of these spiritual truths, and so we need to be reminded of their importance by the spiritual masters.

Suddenly, while reading, things may begin to click together for us on many levels. We see the connecting links between humility, detachment, fraternal charity. We see why from the spiritual perspective the "down moments" of failure and ego desperation can be blessings in disguise, leading us away from self complacency and toward repentance.

Here again, the spiritual reading notebook helps. After keeping it for about six months to a year, we can go back over what we have written and perhaps begin to see a pattern of spiritual selfhood emerging. Certain attitudes become thematic of our whole spiritual life, both attitudes that oppose growth in the spirit, like arrogance, and attitudes that promote this growth, like simplicity and trust in God's care. The notebook may also be a record of the times in which we've spontaneously turned to God in prayer and asked him to help us overcome our resistance to grace.

I remember a student of mine who discovered through the reading notebook that anger was thematic in her life. There were many entries that revealed how this anger extended to the text she was reading and to the spiritual writer who composed it. She even felt angry at times with God. She could not deny that she had written these angry remarks; all she could do was read them over and try gently to grow with God's grace beyond being a predominantly angry person. The notebook helped her to raise her anger to the level of consciousness where she was able to begin to deal with it before God.

For another person trust in God's providence emerged as a life theme; for someone else, the hunger for solitude; for one quiet girl, the need for true involvement in teaching as a way of witnessing for the Lord. All kinds of personal discoveries are possible through keeping a record of the dialogue that occurs between ourselves and the text we are reading.

From all this, it may be clear that spiritual reading can be an important tool for the formation of the true disciple. To the degree that he or she is imbibing this art, its fruits can be communicated to others in the world. We can begin to awaken in them their own capacity for personal reflection before God. We may be instrumental in helping them not only to memorize historical facts but to arouse their dormant powers of creativity in response to the word. Personal appropriation of the Lord's way, truth and life through spiritual reading is instrumental in the development of the disciple; through him others may come in touch with themselves and the God they long to see.

X

From the fig tree learn a lesson. When its branch grows tender and sprouts leaves, you realize that summer is near. Likewise, when you see all these things happening, you will know that he is near, standing at your door. I assure you, the present generation will not pass away until all this takes place. The heavens and the earth will pass away but my words will not pass. (Mt. 24:32-35)

To find self formation by means of scripture reading, I must be open in docility to what its text may eventually tell me about myself; I must abide with formative reading until it yields to me its treasure. Formative reading implies, moreover, my willingness to change my current self in light of the formative insight scripture may radiate to me. The word as formative has the power to transform me. It can give rise to a new self in Christ, permeating all dimensions of my life. The word as formative can lift me beyond the stirrings of my ego and vital life so that I may discover my graced life form in the Eternal Word.

(Adrian van Kaam, *Woman at the Well)*

135

X

THE FORMATIVE ART OF
SPIRITUAL READING

We know from experience that the teacher most vividly remembered by us was often inspiring not because of her words but because of the person she was. Her quality of presence made a lasting impression on us. She may not have been the most brilliant or clever person, but she taught from her heart and could relate to the class on a human level. She loved us and listened to us; she wanted to be where we were and move on from there. She respected the uniqueness of each person because she saw the Lord in each person. Her presence can stay with us for a lifetime, reverberating in us long after the remembrance of other teachers has worn off. So witness value is undeniable.

Today many people, young and old, are looking for a spiritual context that will give some ultimate meaning to their lives. What we can offer them as teachers and disciples of Christ is a chance to meet our Divine Master, who is the beginning and end of their search. Jesus has commissioned us to bring mankind a message of gladness; we begin to fulfill His call by living the Gospel as intently as we can in our homes, schools, offices and churches. We may stumble a bit; we may grope for words, but as we continue to resource ourselves at the wellspring of Christ's words, we can become courageous carriers of His Good News to the world.

One fundamental condition for discipleship is formative spiritual reading, that is, the reading of Holy Scripture or spiritual literature in such a way that it influences my life. I bring myself to the text as I am and try to imbibe its meaning in a personal way.[1]

Formative spiritual reading is attentive to the text at hand as it becomes my "teacher." When I do informational reading, I am more in charge. I often set up a dialogue or comparison between this author and that one, between my own thinking at this time and what the author is telling me. But when I read the text spiritually, I must shift at that moment to an attitude of docility. I move into the mode of discipleship, not so much wanting to teach as to be taught. This shift in attitude indicates that spiritual reading is also less dissective-analytical, less an act of taking the text apart, and more dynamic-synthetic, putting the message of the spiritual writer or poet within the context of my own search for transcendent life meaning.[2]

Emerging as it does from the depths of the spirit, the text may at times lack exact logic due to the fact that the writer is trying to be faithful to his experience of God with all its shadows and ambiguities. Thus we find in spiritual writing and speaking a wise use of paradox. The writer introduces us to a mode of apparent contradiction that is still true to life. The purpose of paradox is to evoke in the disciple an insight that goes beyond ego consciousness. Paradox leads us to an awareness of the mystery of life no reasoning can resolve. Facts that satisfy the logical mind are transcended. The point is not to solve the paradox but to let the unsolvability of it evoke in the disciple a sense of wonder. Objective knowledge divides, dissects and reduces mystery to man's control, but mystery is greater than man and will sooner or later break into and disrupt his complacency. The rational intellect, divorced from faith, can never enter the world of meaning that exists in the invisible realm of the spirit.

Holy Scripture, for example, is filled with paradox:

Whoever would save his life, will lose it, but whoever loses his life for my sake will find it. (Mt. 16:35)

Whoever makes himself lowly, becoming like this child, is of greatest importance in that heavenly reign. (Mt. 18:4)

. . . it is easier for a camel to pass through a needle's eye than for a rich man to enter the kingdom of God. (Mt. 19:24)

The stone which the builders rejected has become the keystone of the structure. (Mt. 21:42)

Jesus wants his disciples to be confronted by paradox so that they can open up to the truth beneath common sense facts and thus grow in wisdom. Paradoxes like these, which reverse human expectations, tell us that we are to abandon ourselves to the Spirit of God despite worldly persecution. The Christian disciple becomes profoundly aware that the foolishness of God is wiser than human wisdom. (1 Co. 1:18-25) Jesus warns His followers that they will have to travel a narrow way. Anyone who lives in the illusion of ease and safety and refuses to take up His cross cannot hope to taste the fruits of the Spirit. As spiritual readers, we must let the formative power of Jesus' words free us from whatever prevents us from following the Father's will in this life.

A first rule of formative reading is *selection.* Imagine being invited by a great king to share in a royal banquet. The table is fantastic—fish, fowl, fruit—the possibilities to choose from are so rich I at first don't know what to take. Decorum tells me to select not too much and not too little. Just the right amount of food, slowly savored, will satisfy me and show the king my appreciation. Something comparable happens in spiritual reading when I choose wisely the nourishment I will receive from the banquet table of Holy Scripture and the writings of the spiritual masters. Selection enables us to tune into the truths hidden in the text. We begin to spiral into the word, to uncover its inner riches.

A second rule of formative reading is that of *rumination*. We, as it were, "chew over" the text taken in by reading. What is it saying to me? How does this saying apply to my life? Why do these words resonate in my soul and how do they affect my relation with God here and now? How can I apply the rich nourishment received in spiritual reading to the day to day situation in which I am living. The text ruminated upon may provide a link between my life, limited as it is, and the directives coming from God through the situation I am in. The "morsel" I have selected thus begins to move into my mind, and deeper still into my heart, fashioning me into the other Christ I am called to be.

A third phase involves *assimilation*. The nourishment we have selected and meditated upon begins to stir in our whole being. We let this encounter with God, evoked by the word, become the ever present background of our life. We pause frequently during the day to bring the text to the forefront of our thoughts. It serves as a pointer to the transcendent and prepares us for those times in prayer when we meet God in explicit ways: to ask him for what we need; to thank him for what he has given us; to praise his name; to tell him of our love; and to reaffirm our desire to do his will. His words, which I have read and meditated upon, seal the bond of our relationship; they bind time to the timeless.

Increasingly fashioned by the word, I orient my

whole life to God. He is the Divine Horizon against which my everyday life unfolds. I open myself to the power of the word to turn my entire life into one long unceasing prayer. I pray for the grace of being open to the inspiration of God from whatever source it comes: a text, the liturgy, another person's witness. My "spiritual radar" is so attuned to God that it picks up and attends to His call whenever and through whomever it comes. This phase of assimislation does not mean doing spectacular things for God but simply living in the hiddenness of ordinary routine—the difference being that my body, mind and heart are raised habitually to God. Such was the case with Brother Lawrence of the Resurrection and St. Therese of the Child Jesus. Prayer for them was not a practice reserved for special occasions but a living reality. Like these saints, we may find ourselves living with God in faith and experiencing His presence in the midst of day to day activity. By practicing the art of formative spiritual reading, we can grow in that deep faith that clings to God in desolation as well as consolation and establishes firmly the bond of intimacy between God and the soul.[3]

A final phase of formative reading fosters *contemplation*. We may find ourselves, along with the spiritual writer, at a loss for words. A certain inner stilling takes hold of us; we feel ourselves being lifted beyond the immediate towards an experience of God's inscrutable transcendence. We are silent before

God and absorbed in his awe-inspiring presence. Our
experience is echoed by St. John of the Cross, who
writes of "An Ecstasy Experienced in High Contemplation."

I entered into unknowing
Yet when I saw myself there
Without knowing where I was
I understood great things;
I shall not say what I felt
For I remained in unknowing
Transcending all knowledge.

That perfect knowledge
Was of peace and holiness
Held at no remove
In profound solitude;
It was something so secret
That I was left stammering
Transcending all knowledge.

I was so whelmed,
So absorbed and withdrawn,
That my senses were left
Deprived of all their sensing,
And my spirit was given
An understanding while not understanding,
Transcending all knowledge.[4]

This experience of "transcending all knowledge" is a pure gift of God. He grants to the disciple the undeserved gift of His divine self communication and draws him toward total surrender. Words give way to silent wonder before the utter fullness of God. One has no further desire to speak as this passage from St. John's *Living Flame of Love* shows:

And in your sweet breathing
Filled with good and glory,
How tenderly You swell my heart with love!

I do not desire to speak of this spiration, filled for the soul with good and glory and delightful love of God, for I am aware of being incapable of so doing, and were I to try, it might seem less than it is. It is a spiration which God produces in the soul, in which, by the awakening of lofty knowledge of the Godhead, He breathes the Holy Spirit in it in the same proportion as its knowledge and understanding of Him, absorbing it most profoundly in the Holy Spirit, rousing its love with divine excellence and delicacy according to what it beholds in Him. Since the breathing is filled with good and glory, the Holy Spirit through this breathing filled the soul with good and glory, in which He enkindled it in love of Himself, indescribably and incomprehensibly in the depths of God, to whom be honor and glory forever and ever.[5]

Drawn into the depths of God, the soul experiences a peace that surpasses all understanding in a breathless moment, suspended between time and eternity. It is God who breathes His own life into the soul. And this

To descend from these transcendent heights is difficult, but we must return to the everyday world. That is why we include as part of formative reading the phase of *participation*. Hopefully our inner vision has been transformed, our attitude refined. Our reading has made us more open to the Spirit in all we say and do. We are able to reset our priorities, making the first aim of life union with God and letting all other activities flow from that intention. Our goal, in other words, is the harmonious blending of earth with heaven, of incarnation with inspiration, of action with vision, of work with worship.

Our good intention to reach, with God's grace, the goal of integration may go awry if we identify spirituality only with spine-tingling feelings or mountain top experiences, as if to say that life in an ordinary family or parish cannot be spiritual. Our life is torn between a vain search for ecstatic heights and the drab life of everyday. This split existence may incline us to the willful invention of pseudo-mystical feelings that hinder our love for the hidden life of the Lord and our readiness to let Him fashion our life. Any "do-it-myself" tendencies may mar the delicate work He is doing in my soul. We forget the fact of our dependence on God and grow self-reliant. Projects of self-salvation replace the recognition that without the Lord I can do nothing. Jesus alone is my savior. I do not take myself up but I am a being who is taken up by God. The self that I am called to be is hidden in Him, utterly indebted to His mercy. He is the source of all human goodness and strength. God is everything. God is all. Led by him to the heights of union, St. John of the Cross had only this to say:

Delight in the world's good things
At the very most
Can only tire the appetite
And spoil the palate;
And so, not for all of sweetness
Will I ever lose myself,
But for I-don't-know-what
Which is so gladly found.

. . .

He who is sick with love,
Whom God Himself has touched,
Finds his tastes so changed
That they fall sway
Like a fevered man's
Who loathes any food he sees
And desires I-don't-know-what
Which is so gladly found.

. . .

For when once the will
Is touched by God Himself
It cannot be satisfied
Except by God;

145

> But since His Beauty is open
> To faith alone, the will
> Tastes Him in I-don't-know-what
> Which is so gladly found.

> . . .

> I will never lose myself
> For that which the senses
> Can take in here,
> Nor for all the mind can hold,
> No matter how lofty,
> Nor for grace or beauty,
> But only for I-don't-know-what
> Which is so gladly found.[6]

In conclusion, what are some of the life attitudes that result from this formative encounter between the self and God on the meeting ground of sacred words?

For one thing, we find that the saints speak of their wretchedness, of how incorrigible they are, of how they are really the worst sinners in the world. When we read their books, we are horrified to hear them say such things of themselves. They seem so holy to us. But in their holiness they become deeply sensitive to any obstacles they put in the way of grace. The more one becomes perfect in Christ, that is, the more one puts on Jesus, the more sensitive he is to what the Lord would say and do in every situation. Griping, negativity, ingratitude gradually disappear as God perfects with His grace the image of Himself He wants us to be.

Another repercussion of the transformation process seems to be an increased vitality, along with a keener functionality. For example, when we read the life of St. Teresa of Avila, we are amazed by her energy and practicality. Until the end of her life, she was active in establishing new foundations of Carmel, despite her many physical ailments and her passive reception of mystical graces.[7] The author of *The Cloud of Unknowing* also comments upon the transformed countenance of the person who lives a deep interior life. He or she radiates the gracious, gentle presence of Christ that any person can be responsive to.[8] Even if the holy person is physically unattractive, this sense of the Sacred living in him comes through.

Unquestionably, a mark of the transformed self is inner peace. The saints manifest the grace of equanimity, that faithful capacity to flow with delight or aridity, desolation or consolation—with whatever God wills. This evenness of mood, this tranquility and peace, are unmistakable marks of the person who lives in Christ; he is a channel through which the wisdom of Holy Scripture and the spiritual masters can spread from age to age, encompassing all generations. What is yet to be revealed to us in the life to come remains unknown, but even on earth we can live in the light that prompted the poet Gerard Manley Hopkins to proclaim:

The world is charged with the grandeur of God.
It will flame out, like shining from shook foil;

RENEWED AT EACH AWAKENING

It gathers to a greatness, like the ooze of oil
Crushed. Why do men then now not reck his rod?
Generations have trod, have trod, have trod;
    And all is seared with trade; bleared, smeared with
      toil;
    And wears man's smudge and shares man's smell: the
      soil
    Is bare now, nor can foot feel, being shod.

And for all this, nature is never spent;
    There lives the dearest freshness deep down things;
And though the last lights off the black West went
    Oh, morning, at the brown brink eastward, springs—
Because the Holy Ghost over the bent
    World broods with warm breast and with ah! bright
      wings.[9]

SUGGESTED READING LIST
IN THE LITERATURE OF SPIRITUALITY

The Catholic Christian Tradition
Compiled by Dr. S.A. Muto

Holy Scripture

Old Testament

Pentateuch—Genesis, Exodus, Deuteronomy

The Historical Books—1 Samuel, 2 Samuel, 1 Kings,
2 Kings

The Wisdom Books—Job, Psalms, Proverbs, Ecclesiastes,
Song of Songs, Wisdom, Sirach

The Prophetic Books—Isaiah, Jeremiah, Lamentations,
Ezekiel, Hosea, Jonah, Habakkuk, Zechariah

New Testament

Entire Collection

Literature of Spirituality

The Patristic Age

Benedicta Ward, Trans., *The Sayings of the Desert Fathers*
Thomas Merton, *The Wisdom of the Desert*
J.K. Ryan, Trans., *The Confessions of St. Augustine*
Abbot Justin McCann, Ed., *The Rule of St. Benedict*
Pseudo-Dionysius, *The Divine Names and the Mystical Theology*
Aelred Squire, *Asking the Fathers*

The Middle Ages

Sermons

Bernard of Clairvaux *Sermons on the Song of Songs* and in
Treatises II—The Steps of Humanity and Pride and *On
Loving God*

149

RENEWED AT EACH AWAKENING

Aelred of Rievaulx, *Spiritual Friendship*

William of St. Thierry, *The Golden Epistle*

Walter Farrell and Martin Healy, *My Way of Life* (The Summa of St. Thomas Aquinas Simplified for Everyone)

St. Catherine of Siena, *The Dialogue*

St. Francis of Assisi, *The Little Flowers of St. Francis*

St. Bonaventure, *The Journey of the Soul to God* (Itinerarium Mentis in Deum)

R.B. Blakney, Trans., *Meister Eckhart* (A Modern Translation)

John Ruysbroeck, *The Adornment of Spiritual Marriage*

Thomas à Kempis. *The Imitation of Christ*

Walter Hilton, *The Scale of Perfection*

Richard Rolle, *The Fire of Love*

Anonymous, *The Cloud of Unknowing* (Wm. Johnston, Ed.)

Julian of Norwich, *The Revelations of Divine Love*

St. Catherine of Genoa, *A Dialogue between the Soul and the Body*

Modern Times (16th to 19th Century)

Augustine Baker, *Holy Wisdom*

St. Ignatius of Loyola, *The Spiritual Exercises of St. Ignatius*

St. Teresa of Avila, *The Autobiography of St. Teresa of Avila; The Way of Perfection; The Interior Castle*

St. John of the Cross, *The Collected Works of St. John of the Cross:* The Ascent of Mount Carmel; The Dark Night; The Spiritual Canticle; The Living Flame of Love; Sayings of Light and Love

St. Therese of Lisieux, *Story of a Soul; Collected Letters; Last Conversations*

Bro. Lawrence, *The Practice of the Presence of God*

Jean Pierre de Caussade, *Abandonment to Divine Providence*

Jean Nicholas Grou, *How to Pray*

St. Francis de Sales, *Introduction to the Devout Life; Treatise on the Love of God*

Adrian van Kaam, *A Light to the Gentiles* (the Life of Ven. Francis Libermann)

Francis Libermann, *Spiritual Letters*

St. Alphonsus Liguori, *Ascetical Works; The Glories of Mary*

E. Kadloubovsky & G.E.H. Palmer, Trans., *Writings from the Philokalia on Prayer of the Heart*

Anonymous, *The Way of the Pilgrim and the Pilgrim Continues His Way*

Jean Baptist de Chautard, *The Soul of the Apostolate*

Dom Marmion, *Christ, the Life of the Soul; Christ in HIs Mysteries*

John Henry Newman, *Apologia Pro Vita Sua*

John Woolman, *The Journal of John Woolman*

Henry David Thoreau, *Walden*

Modern Times (20th Century)

Jacques Fesch, *Light Upon the Scaffold: The Prison Letters of Jacques Fesch*

Pope John XXIII, *The Journal of Pope John XXIII*

A. Delp, *The Prison Meditations of Father Delp*

Thomas Merton, *The Seven Storey Mountain; The Sign of Jonas; Seeds of Contemplation; Contemplative Prayer; The Monastic Journey*

Basil Pennington, *O Holy Mountain!*

George Maloney, *Inward Stillness; Bright Darkness*

Walter Ciszek, *With God in Russia; He Leadeth Me*

E. Underhill, *Practical Mysticism*

S. Kierkegaard, *Purity of Heart Is to Will One Thing; The Prayers of Kierkegaard*

T.S. Eliot, *The Wasteland and Other Poems; Four Quartets; Murder in the Cathedral*

Gerard Manley Hopkins, *A Hopkins Reader*

Hannah Hurnard, *Hinds' Feet on High Places*

RENEWED AT EACH AWAKENING

Simone Weil, *Waiting for God*

Martin Buber, *Tales of the Hasidim*

A Little Brother of Jesus, *Silent Pilgrimage to God* (The Life and Writings of Charles de Foucauld)

Dag Hammarskjöld. *Markings*

Thomas Kelly, *A Testament of Devotion*

Anne Morrow Lindberg, *Gift from the Sea*

Loren Eiseley, *The Unexpected Universe*

Blaise Pascal, *Les Pensees*

Nikos Kazantzakis. *Report to Greco; Zorba the Greek*

Max Picard, *The World of Silence*

Anthony Bloom, *Beginning to Pray; Living Prayer*

Peter van Breemen, *Called by Name*

C.S. Lewis, *A Grief Observed; Surprised by Joy*

Anne Frank, *Diary of a Young Girl*

F. Dostovesky, *The Brothers Karamazov*

G. Bernados, *Diary of a Country Priest*

Carlo Carretto, *Letters from the Desert; Summoned by Love*

Adrian van Kaam, *Spirituality and the Gentle Life; Woman at the Well; Looking for Jesus*

Adrian van Kaam and Susan Muto, *Am I Living a Spiritual Life*

Susan Muto, *Approaching the Sacred; Steps Along the Way; The Journey Homeward*

For further reference see: Susan Muto, *A Practical Guide to Spiritual Reading* and David A. Fleming, *The Fire and the Cloud* (Anthology)

FOOTNOTES

PART ONE

FOREWORD

1. Dag Hammarskjöld, *Markings,* Trans. W.H. Auden (London: Faber and Faber, 1964), p. 101.
2. Quotations from Holy Scripture are taken usually from *The Jerusalem Bible,* Reader's Edition (Garden City, N.Y.: Doubleday & Company, Inc., 1971).

CHAPTER ONE

1. See Adrian van Kaam, *On Being Yourself: Reflections on Spirituality and Originality* (Denville, N.J.: Dimension Books, 1972).

2. Dag Hammarskjöld, *Markings,* Trans. W.H. Auden (London: Faber and Faber, 1964), pp. 139-140.

CHAPTER II

1. See Adrian van Kaam and Susan Annette Muto, *Am I Living a Spiritual Life?* (Denville, N.J.: Dimension Books, 1978).

2. See Adrian van Kaam, *Spirituality and the Gentle Life* (Denville, N.J.: Dimension Books, 1974).

CHAPTER III

1. Adrian van Kaam, Bert van Croonenburg, Susan Muto, *The Emergent Self* (Denville, N.J.: Dimension Books, 1968), p. 24.

2. See Adrian van Kaam, *Dynamics of Spiritual Self Direction* (Denville, N.J.: Dimension Books, 1976).

3. *The Confessions of St. Augustine,* trans. John K. Ryan (New York: Image Books, 1960), Book 1, Chapter 1, p. 43.

4. *The Collected Works of St. John of the Cross,* trans. Kieran Kavanaugh and Otilio Rodriguez (Washington, D.C.: Institute of Carmelite Studies, 1973), p. 671.

5. Nikos Kazantzakis, *Zorba the Greek* (New York: Ballantine Books, 1964), pp. 138-39.

CHAPTER IV

1. Viktor Frankl, *Man's Search for Meaning* (New York: Washington Square Press, 1964).

2. See Elisabeth Kubler-Ross, *On Death and Dying* (New York: Macmillan, 1970).

3. Bradford Smith, *Dear Gift of Life* (Pendle Hill Pamphlet, Lebanon, Pa.: Sowers Printing Co., 1965), p. 31.

4. Smith, pp. 5-7.

5. Ibid., p. 7.

6. Ibid. p. 15.

7. Dietrich Bonhoeffer, *Letters & Papers from Prison* (New York: Macmillan, 1972), pp. 370-371.

8. Smith, p. 22.

CHAPTER V

1. I am indebted to Adrian van Kaam for this description of the spiritual life.

2. *The Collected Works of St. John of the Cross,* p. 673.

3. Ibid., p. 543.

4. Thomas Merton, *Thoughts in Solitude* (New York: Image Books, 1968), p. 93.

5. *The Collected Works of St. John of the Cross,* Ascent of Mount Carmel, Book 1, Chapter 11, Paragraph 4, p. 97.

6. Merton, p. 103.

7. See *The Way of Perfection,* trans. E. Allison Peers (New York, Image Books, 1964).

8. Nikos Kazantzakis, *Report to Greco* (New York: Bantam Books, 1966), pp. 279-80.

9. *The Collected Works of St. John of the Cross,* p. 675.

10. Merton, p. 84.

11. *The Savings of the Desert Fathers,* Trans. Benedicta Ward (Kalamazoo, Michigan: Cistercian Publications, 1975), #27, p. 6.

12. See Susan Annette Muto, "Solitude, Self-Presence and True Participation," *Spiritual Life* (Volume 20, Number 4, Winter, 1974), pp. 231-37.

PART TWO

CHAPTER VI

1. T.S. Eliot, "Choruses from 'The Rock,' " in *The Complete Poems and Plays, 1909-1950* (New York: Harcourt, Brace, Jovanovich, Inc., 1952), p. 96.

2. *The Confessions of St. Augustine,* trans. John K. Ryan (New York: Image Books, 1960), Book 8, Chapter 12, p. 202.

3. "Choruses from 'The Rock,' " p. 104.

4. Thomas Merton, *The Sign of Jonas* (New York: Image Books, 1956), pp. 116-17.

CHAPTER VIII

1. See Susan Annette Muto, *Approaching the Sacred: An Introduction to Spiritual Reading* (Denville, N.J.: Dimension Books, 1973).

2. T.S. Eliot, *Four Quartets,* in *The Complete Poems and Plays, 1909-1950* (New York: Harcourt, Brace, Jovanovich, Inc., 1952), p. 128.

CHAPTER IX

1. Walt Whitman, *Selections from Leaves of Grass* (New York: Avenel Books, 1961), p. 86.

2. T.S. Eliot, *Four Quartets,* in *The Complete Poems and Plays, 1909-1950* (New York: Harcourt, Brace, Jovanovich, Inc., 1952), p. 127.

CHAPTER X

1. See Adrian van Kaam, *Woman at the Well* (Denville, N.J.: Dimension Books, 1977) and *Looking for Jesus* (Denville, N.J.: Dimension Books, 1978).

2. See Susan Annette Muto, *Steps Along the Way: The Path of Spiritual Reading* (Denville, N.J.: Dimension Books, 1975) and *A Practical Guide to Spiritual Reading* (Denville, N.J.: Dimension Books, 1976).

3. See Susan Annette Muto, *The Journey Homeward: On the Road of Spiritual Reading* (Denville, N.J.: Dimension Books, 1977).

4. From *The Collected Works of St. John of the Cross,* trans. Kieran Kavanaugh and Otilio Rodriguez (Washington, D.C.: Institute of Carmelite Studies, 1973). See pp. 718-19 for the entire poem.

5. *The Collected Works,* p. 649.

6. See *The Collected Works,* pp. 735-36 for the entire poem.

7. See *The Collected Works of St. Teresa of Avila,* Volume One, trans. Kieran Kavanaugh and Otilio Rodriguez (Washington, D.C.: Institute of Carmelite Studies, 1976).

8. See *The Cloud of Unknowing,* trans. Clifton Wolters (Baltimore: Penguin Books, 1961).

9. Gerard Manley Hopkins, *Poems and Prose,* Ed. W.H. Gardner (Baltimore: Penguin Books, 1953), p. 27.